To those who search…

PASSPORT TO WORSHIPPING

IN SPIRIT AND IN TRUTH

« I will build you a house »

Mikaël REALE

Illustration: **Mare Nostrum Project**
© 2020 Mikaël REALE

Published by : BoD—Books on Demand
12/14 rond-point des Champs Elysées
75008 Paris FRANCE
Printed by BoD – Books on Demand,
Norderstedt

ISBN : 9782322205073

Legal registration : Mai 2020

INTRODUCTION

For some years now, the term "Tabernacle of David" has been embraced whole-heartedly by the world of evangelical Christians, and especially so in charismatic groups. We are seeing more and more churches who are discovering or rediscovering the importance of praise and worship in their meetings and who are now organising meetings entirely for the purpose of worship.

And it is true: what could be more natural than to consecrate some of our meetings exclusively to God the Father, the Son and the Holy Spirit!

All over, teams of worshippers are gathering for 24-hour non-stop "Tabernacle of David" meetings.

This passion for praise and worship seems to me to be the result of a prophetic breath preparing for the return of Jesus Christ. Does the Bible not tell us that God is seated in the midst of the praises of His people?

But in order for this zeal not to be merely yet another fashion amongst Christians, I believe it is important to understand what praise and worship actually is. What is its purpose? How does it honour God? But more than that, what is at stake spiritually?

To understand this, we need to realise that since the beginning of creation, worship has existed, and the one who was put in charge of it was an angel named Lucifer, who after his fall, would become Satan!

Today, as people bought at a price, we are called to take up the place that Satan lost – that of bringing worship to the Lord. We have every reason, therefore, to be apprehensive of the spiritual battle resulting from this function entrusted to the Church.

Satan has certainly understood this issue, and that is why he is so keen to have the whole world bowing at his feet. He is even willing to give everything he possesses to get us to do this.

Let's read together Matthew 4 vs 8 and 9: *"Again, the devil took him to a very high mountain and showed him all the kingdoms of the world and their splendour. 'All of this I will give you,' he said, 'if you will bow down and worship me.'"*

You and I know that all the earth belongs to Jesus Christ (Psalm 2), but we know, too, that for a set time, they were given to Satan (Luke 4 vs 6, John 12 vs 31).

We need to understand what this represents. The authority that Satan has over the nations allows him to keep some in the most extreme poverty, to fling one lot of people against another in bloody wars, to promote abortion, homosexuality, drugs, alcohol, prostitution throughout the world; to allow Islam to develop at a pace in the Arab world or the most selfish kind of materialism in the West! And he is willing to give up all of his power over the nations if we are prepared to worship him!

If all this is true, there must be a very good reason for it. In spite of his hatred for mankind created in God's image, the devil is prepared to allow those who worship him to prosper. Not because he loves them, but because he derives his very reason for being from their worship.

In the garden of Eden, before the fall, Adam and Eve were themselves an act of permanent worship to God, simply by being the perfect handiwork of God that had not yet been soiled. It was only after their fall that worship would become a sacrifice and would need to cost those who worship.

The Law of Moses would later institute sacrifices, and King David, submitted to the Spirit of God, would set apart men consecrated to maintain a state of worship permanently at the centre of the people of Israel.

Jesus, the perfect man, without sin, is Himself a permanent act of worship to God, as was Adam before the fall, and in all things, He worships His Heavenly Father.

But He goes even further than that since He becomes the complete Sacrifice! This implies that the victim is entirely consecrated to God; the offering that Jesus brings to the Father is, thus, an absolute gift of Himself, the visible sign of the magnitude of His worship to the Father. He brings together the worship from His perfect being in the very way that the Father had intended before sin came into the picture - the kind that costs - in the way God instituted after the fall.

Through His life of total worship, Jesus teaches the Church its role of "the Kingdom of those who sacrifice" as described in Revelation chapter 1, verses 4 - 6: *"John, To the seven churches in the province of Asia: Grace and peace to you from him who is, and who was, and who is to come, and from the seven spirits before his throne, and from Jesus Christ, who is the faithful witness, the firstborn from the dead, and the ruler of the kings of the earth. To him who loves us and has freed us from our sins by his blood, and has made us to be a kingdom and priests to serve his God and Father – to him be glory and power for ever and ever! Amen."*

This position makes us, today, the main enemies of the devil. He cannot bear us taking his place in worship. This is why he will do everything in his power to stop us from entering into our calling of being those who bring a sacrifice.

WHAT IS WORSHIP?

It is the expected, normal manner of communication, established by God Himself from the beginning of time. It is a fundamental principle of the Kingdom of Heaven and never, ever has it been something that was created by man to honour God. It is, therefore, the appropriate, fitting way of expressing ourselves in our relationship with the Creator! It is also the way the three persons of the Trinity communicate with each other.

This means we can then assume that God Himself engages in worship.

He honours His Son in Matt 3 vs 17: *"And a voice from heaven said, 'This is my Son, whom I love; with him I am well pleased,'"* or again, in chapter 17 vs 5: *"While he was still speaking, a bright cloud enveloped them, and a voice from the cloud said, 'This is my Son, whom I love; with him I am well pleased. Listen to him!'"* This is very clearly worship.

Jesus does the same towards the Father in Luke 11 vs 21, in the "Our Father" which begins with worshipping God the Father: *"hallowed be your name!"*, just as He says when speaking of the Holy Spirit in John 16 vs 13 and 14: *"But when he, the Spirit of truth, comes, he will guide you into all truth. He will not speak on his own; he will speak only what he hears, and he will tell you what is yet to come. He will bring glory to me by taking from what is mine and make it known to you."*

There are many other passages that can't all be noted here.

It is worth noting that worship is also the manner of communication that is used in the relationship between nature and its creator. Isaiah 44 vs 23: *"Sing for joy, oh heavens, for the Lord has done this; shout aloud, oh Earth beneath. Burst into song, you mountains, you forests and all your trees, for the Lord has redeemed Jacob; he displays his glory in Israel."*

We can therefore define worship in the kingdom of god as being the natural way of communicating in our relationship with god

God wants to restore a relationship between us and Him according to *His* relationship norms, not ours! This means we can be sure of the fact that right from the first chapters of Genesis and all through the Bible, that the Lord is a God of relationship. Let's read together a few verses from Genesis 2.

Verse 18: *"The Lord God said, 'It is not good for the man to be alone. I will make a helper suitable for him.'"* Contemplating the human being, God realises that he can't be alone. God does not wonder about this problem with regard to the rest of His creation, but only in respect of the one He made in His image, and who, thus, has similar needs to his Creator's.

God, therefore, decides to give Adam a spouse who will be his "helper" and in so doing, brings in the first institution that will govern relationships between men: Marriage. *"For this reason, a man will leave his father and mother and be united to his wife, and they will become one flesh."* (Verse 24)

During all of the first few chapters of Genesis, we see that God regularly visits man. He engages with Adam to see what he will call the animals, when evening comes. He comes to visit the first couple. God is an integral part of their life. In fact, the relationship between the two spouses is based on worship. *"The man said, 'This is bone of my bones and flesh of my flesh; she shall be called "woman" for she was taken out of man.'"* (Genesis 2:23)

But alas, the first sin of an interminable list intervened. We know all of its spiritual consequences: Romans 6 vs 23: *"For the wages of sin is death"*, but I want to draw your attention to the immediate consequence today resulting from this, in terms of human relationships.

Having declared that woman was flesh of his flesh, bone of his bones, Adam completely dissociated himself from her in terms of their responsibility. In verse 12 of chapter 3, we read: *"The woman you put here with me – she gave me some fruit from the tree, and I ate it."*

In other words, it's not my fault; it is the woman's! Not **MY** wife, but **THE** wife that **YOU** gave me. So, it's your fault, not mine!

From this moment, human relationships would become poisoned, the first fratricide, Cain and Abel, then wars, murders, genocides, abortion, suicide, etc…

The relationship between man and God experiences the consequences of sin too. Firstly, fear comes in. Verse 10: *"I heard you in the garden, and I was afraid because I was naked; so I hid."* Then a relationship perverted by pride, that leads God not to accept the sacrifice offered by Cain, ultimately Cain's rebellion, as rather than accepting God's recommendations that are full of love, he throws off restraint, abandons himself to sin and rebellion, and assassinates his brother.

But God has a plan allowing Him to restore this relationship. He throws a bridge over the gulf that Satan dug between Him and humanity. That bridge is in the shape of the cross of Calvary.

It is thanks to this that we have eternal life, Romans 5 vs 10: *"For if, when we were God's enemies, we were reconciled to him through the death of his Son, how much more, having been reconciled, shall we be saved through his life?"*

It goes without saying that Satan is not pleased to see the relationship with God and with the rest of humanity being restored in Christ! The two main reasons for his anger are the following:

He is jealous and behaves like a kindergarten child who has broken his toy and so decides to break another child's toy. He can't bear the fact that we have taken his place, even if he himself doesn't want to fulfil this task anymore.

Then, and tragically so, he understands a whole lot better than many Christians what is at stake when it comes to worship!

Satan knows that when we worship God, we come before the throne of grace, and it is there that God will bless us, heal us, equip us for battle, and give us His "MISSION ORDERS" so that we can rise up against the devil and his demons to take back our heritage! Satan knows it is through worship that we are victorious. Psalm 18 vs 3: *"I call to the Lord, who is worthy of praise, and I am saved from my enemies."* He will thus fight to make sure we are not able to enter fully into worship.

COMING OUT OF EGYPT

A good example of what this battle may entail can be seen in the first chapters of Exodus. We will read a few passages and then discuss them.

To begin with, let's ask ourselves the following question: What is the reason Moses asks Pharaoh to be allowed to leave Egypt? We read the answer to this in *Exodus 5 vs 1: "Afterwards, Moses and Aaron went to Pharaoh and said, 'This is what the Lord, the God of Israel, says: Let my people go, so that they may hold a festival to me in the desert.'"*

The first thing to note is that we see God expects His people to celebrate Him, whereas Pharaoh, who symbolises Satan, affirms that he does not know God. *"Pharaoh said, 'Who is this Lord, that I should obey him and let Israel go? I do not know the Lord and I will not let Israel go.'"* And under this pretext, he refuses to allow Israel to offer God the worship due to Him.

This reminds me of some situations that we find ourselves in when our families or our friends are not converted. These people don't understand why we go to a worship service on a Sunday morning instead of staying in bed. They do not understand that we are making God the priority of our lives.

A young woman once admitted to me that her parents, who lived above them, had never said a word when, as a young couple, they would come back at 4am to carry on partying noisily with friends in their lounge.

A few months after the conversion of this couple, these same parents kicked up a huge fuss about the noise they made when they were worshipping the Lord in their garden at 21h45 during a home cell meeting!

But let's get back to Pharaoh. He goes further than that. He makes sure that Israel cannot in any way worship their God, and in verse 9 of the same chapter, he decides: *"Make the work harder for the men so that they keep working and pay no attention to lies."*

The following thing confronts us when we want to worship God. Satan piles a host of things on us to tempt us away from our worship. Sometimes, these are activities: soccer club, a film on TV, a school parents' meeting, a meal out with Aunty Mary... There will always be something better, something more urgent, more "constructive" to do rather than worshipping God if we listen to Satan.

In some cases, these things can even seem to be very spiritual, like frantic activity in the church – an excessive burden in the ministry, the sacrosanct Sunday morning message... I am always staggered to see the ratio of what we do for God compared with what we do for people in what we call "the worship service".

Of the two hours, we average about 45 minutes for a time of designated worship, but very often, the major part of this is there to prepare the people's hearts for the pastor's message, to unwind, to recharge their batteries. In the end, a miniscule portion is left for the One who is meant to be receiving our worship.

A pastor friend once said to me: "It is the only time in the week that we have the people in our hands; if we don't preach then, if we don't teach, if we don't do the announcements, when do you want us to do all of that?" In fact, our worship services on a Sunday are not worship services at all; they are get-togethers for Christians. Useful – certainly – but they are not worship services.

A few years ago, when I was on a year's Sabbatical, having spent 6 years in the mission field practically without a break, the Lord asked me the following question: *"Where have you been, son?"* I was really shocked by this question, seeing as I had sacrificed my whole life and my family's, to serve God in the Indian Ocean region. It took me a moment to realise that the real question was not about the place or even the things I had done, but on the quality of my relationship with God. *Where had I been as a SON[1]?*

More than what we are doing for God, it is what we are to Him that interests Him!

When this issue of priorities is sorted out in our lives, Satan harasses us in a different way. Haven't you ever noticed how the phone will ring just as you are settling down to have your quiet time with the Lord, or how the kids will get sick the very evening there is a night of prayer at church? Or how some idiot behind the wheel will swerve in front of you on a Sunday morning on your way to church and you sit there during the meeting with your nerves on edge, unable to focus your attention on worshipping God? That is why it sometimes becomes necessary to take "time off" to be able to worship God.

Separation from the world

In our present world, worshipping God the same way as in the polytheistic world in the time of Moses, implies often having to remove ourselves for a time from our daily normal routine.

We see this when we read Exodus 8 vs 25-27: *"Then Pharaoh summoned Moses and Aaron and said, 'Go, sacrifice to your God here in the land.' But Moses said, 'That would not be right. The sacrifices we offer the Lord our God would be detestable to the Egyptians. And if we offer sacrifices that are detestable in their eyes, will they not stone us? We must take a three-day journey into the desert to offer sacrifices to the Lord our God, as he commands us.'"*

Worshipping God inevitably leads us to separate ourselves from the things that we are sometimes attached to. Actually, worship is a spiritual thing, and so by its very nature, it is opposed to our flesh. Galatians 5 vs 17 affirms: *"For the sinful nature desires what is contrary to the Spirit, and the Spirit what is contrary to the sinful nature. They are in conflict with each other, so that you do not do what you want."*

Just as the flesh will not appreciate walking for three days in the desert, it won't appreciate getting up early on a Sunday morning after a week at work either, to go and sing some songs at church. It also doesn't appreciate our friends mocking us. Oh yay! You're off to mass... It does not appreciate us having to break up with our fiancé(e) or sometimes even with our partner or spouse.

Satan will try to manipulate us cleverly physically and emotionally by impressing on us: *"Pharaoh said, 'The Lord be with you – if I let you go along with your women and children! Clearly you are bent on evil.'" Exodus 10:10*

It is not enjoyable to worship God, if we listen to our flesh, and it is a real sacrifice not to listen to what our flesh says, as we are carnal.

We need to understand something important here with regard to human nature. Man, who was created in the image of God, consists of three elements, each with its own reason for being. The body, the soul and the spirit. This is true for everyone, converted or not.

In 1 Thessalonians 5 vs 23, we read: *"May God Himself, the God of peace, sanctify you through and through. May your whole spirit, soul and body be kept blameless at the coming of our Lord Jesus Christ."*

One of the issues that we often face in our Christian lives is the confusion between the spirit and the soul. This issue crops up particularly in the area of worship, where we too often strive with our souls to motivate ourselves to worship, when actually, the source of worship is to be found in our spirit which is always seeking to have a real relationship with God.

I sometimes hear messages teaching that God is seeking our worship. In fact, some people just want to do that. Others will emphasise the quality of the music, the last word when it comes to sound, the perfection of the choreography... But in fact, God has nothing to do with all of those. He is not looking for worship; He is looking for worshippers!

Remember these words of Jesus: *"Yet a time is coming and has now come when the true worshippers will worship the Father in spirit and truth!" (John 4 vs 23)*

What does this actually mean?

In spirit means that our spiritual nature, our spirit that has been born again in Jesus Christ, longs to meet with its Creator so that an intimate relationship may be established between the two of them.

In truth means that as a result of this intimate relationship with God, our lives will be transformed, so that every day, they will be in phase with Jesus. In other words, we can no longer live, think and act in the same way!

Our Worship needs to be total!

When you have eventually gone through these different stages to get into worship, you have already taken a big step. The battle, however, is not over yet.

Satan will now try to limit your worship as we read in the following verses, by separating the people.
Exodus 10 vs 1: *"'No! Have only the men go and worship the Lord, since that's what you have been asking for.' Then Moses and Aaron were driven out of Pharaoh's presence."*

It is absolutely essential for God's people to stay together to worship! Satan often begins by tempting to sow division in the church during the service.

Because of someone who didn't greet somebody else, someone else who sat in my usual place…
or because of another person whom I really don't appreciate or whom I suspect doesn't appreciate me… because the bass guitar is too loud, or because a particular guitarist is leading the worship even though he is less spiritual than I am, etc.

We can find a thousand and one reasons to separate ourselves, but not one of these reasons can be more important than the one who unites us: JESUS CHRIST!

Satan will also try to limit our worship by stopping us bringing sacrifices to God.

Let's now read Exodus 10 vs 24-26: *"Then Pharaoh summoned Moses and said, 'Go, worship the Lord. Even your women and children may go with you; leave only your flocks and herds behind.' But Moses said, 'You must allow us to have sacrifices and burnt offerings to present to the Lord our God. Our livestock too must go with us; not a hoof is to be left behind. We have to use some of them in worshipping the Lord our God, and until we get there, we will not know what we are to use to worship the Lord.' "*

Without a sacrifice, we have seen that there is no worship. God expects us to put all our trust in Him, and whatever the situation, we need to be prepared to give Him all, in an act of adoration.

We have an impressive example of this in Genesis in the story of the sacrifice of Isaac:

Genesis 22 vs 1 and 2: *"Some time later God tested Abraham. He said to him, 'Abraham!' 'Here I am,' he replied. Then God said, 'Take your son, your only son Isaac, whom you love, and go to the region of Moriah. Sacrifice him there as a burnt offering on one of the mountains I will tell you about.' "*

As you know, God did not take Isaac's life. But Abraham did not know this when he set off. However, his faith in God was such and his trust so great that he was ready to obey the Lord in everything.

Even though today, we no longer have to offer a blood sacrifice to God in order to worship Him, since Jesus gave His life once and for all, we can sacrifice ourselves. Romans 12 vs 1: *"Therefore, I urge you, brothers, in view of God's mercy, to offer your bodies as living sacrifices, holy and pleasing to God – which is your spiritual worship."*

When the Israelites sacrificed a bull, they were giving the tool they used for their labour. When they gave oil or flour, they were giving their food, and when they offered a sheep, they were offering the wool they would use for clothes. All of these, they gave over and above their tithe. How sad to see people so often today coming empty-handed!

I am convinced that this is as important in His eyes as lifting up beautiful prayers to heaven, or singing wonderful songs to Him while lifting our hands up to Him. God expects us to obey Him. That is a pleasing offering to Him. But over and above that, He expects us to demonstrate our faith by showing that our trust is in Him, rather than in our possessions.

I believe with all my heart that it is impossible for us to worship the Father in spirit and in truth, as Jesus commanded us in John 4 vs 23, if in our daily lives, we deprive God of the trust we owe Him in areas like tithes and offerings.

Worshipping in truth also means moving in agreement with what we proclaim in our praise and worship. How can one proclaim "Jehovah Jireh" – God our provider - and then deprive God of our offerings because we are afraid of not having enough!

In the book of the prophet Malachi 3 vs 8 – 12, God says: *"But you ask, 'How do we rob you?' In tithes and offerings. You are under a curse – the whole nation of you – because you are robbing me. Bring the whole tithe into the storehouse, that there may be food in my house. Test me in this,' says the Lord Almighty, 'and see if I will not throw open the floodgates of heaven and pour out so much blessing that you will not have room enough for it. I will prevent pests from devouring your crops, and the vines in your fields will not cast their fruit,' says the Lord Almighty. 'Then all the nations will call you blessed, for yours will be a delightful land,' says the Lord Almighty."*

This is the only time in the Bible that God asks us to put Him to the test. If God does it, it is because our disobedience in this area must really be an obstacle in His desire to bless us.

It is clear in context of the New Testament that we are no longer subject to the same legalistic ways of the Old Testament. We have passed to a new thing. But not being subject to a law does not mean that the principle of that law is not right.

In the First Testament, up until the Holy Spirit was poured out over everyone on the day of Pentecost, only kings, prophets and priests received the anointing of the Holy Spirit. The laws were thus necessary for the people to be blessed, within the framework of spiritual principles such as this one spoken of in Malachi.

But when the Holy Spirit was poured out, the written laws no longer had a reason to exist, since God Himself wrote His law in our hearts.

Today, we are not called to follow the written law, but rather, we are called to allow the law to live in us through Christ.

Paul explains this very clearly in his letter to the Galatians in chapter 2 vs 20 - 21: *"I have been crucified with Christ, and I no longer live, but Christ lives in me. I do not set aside the grace of God, for if righteousness could be gained through the law, Christ died for nothing."*

Just as the son of God did, it is only at the cost of total sacrifice, letting go of our own will to do His will, that we can bring worship before God that is pleasing to Him.

In Luke 22: 42, Jesus shows us what our worship has to be. *"Father, if you are willing, take this cup from me; yet not my will but yours be done."*

No real worship without been "Born Again"

Finally, we see that in order to enter into worship, Israel had to go through one more stage, and this one was not the work of Pharaoh. Exodus 12: 21 – 24: *"Then Moses summoned all the elders of Israel and said to them, 'Go at once and select the animals for your families and slaughter the Passover lamb. Take a bunch of hyssop, dip it into the blood in the basin and put some of the blood on the top and on both sides of the door-frame. Not one of you shall go out of the door of his house until morning. When the Lord goes through the land to strike down the Egyptians, He will see the blood on the top and sides of the door-frame and will pass over that doorway, and He will not permit the destroyer to enter your houses and strike you down. Obey these instructions as a lasting ordinance for you and your descendants."*

The only thing that allows us to come freely before the throne of God today to worship and adore Him is the blood of the Passover Lamb of the New Covenant. Without the sacrifice of Jesus on the cross, there is no way we could ever present ourselves before God, as His holiness would consume us. If we can now do so in absolute freedom, then those around us may also do so. It is thus important never to judge someone when they are worshipping the Lord. Some do so with tears, others with shouts of joy, others with loud singing accompanied by modern instruments, whereas others prefer to do so in a more contemplative style. Others worship God through dance, clapping their hands, whereas others prefer to kneel down or lie on the ground in absolute silence. What does it matter what my neighbour is doing! And what does it matter what the brothers and sisters from the next church are doing! For *"where the Spirit of the Lord is, there is freedom." 2 Cor 3: 17.*

How often have I grieved the Holy Spirit by being judgemental! I remember once, in a free evangelical church quite close to the reformed church, being visited powerfully by the Holy Spirit who drew my attention to the face of a granny, while I was finding the time of worship very long and dull, being used to a far more dynamic style of worship in my church. Her face was radiating with such intensity, I realised immediately that this granny was before her God in a moment of what I call "intimate" worship.

The Holy Spirit challenged me severely about my thoughts: "You who are judging these people about how they are worshipping, you have not yet worshipped the Lord for a single second since the service began. You have weighed up the quality of their songs, you have watched them, but now they are before my throne and there you are, sitting in your pew!"

I can guarantee you that since that day, I have not passed judgment on the way my brothers and sisters in Christ worship and when Satan tries to draw my attention to something else rather than God during the worship, I redouble my efforts to keep my eyes fixed on the glory of Jesus.

[1 By the same author: Passport to a New Identity in Christ]

WORSHIP IN CHURCH MEETINGS

When we are led to lead worship, it is important always to have in mind that worship is directed to God and to Him alone. This implies that we should ask the Holy Spirit to teach us the right way to experience and to lead the time of worship during our meetings. Too often, we have an erroneous or incomplete understanding of what these times are meant or are not meant to be. Worship should not be:

- A nice way of uniting the brethren while waiting for the meeting to begin.
- A time to unwind spiritually after a hard week at work.
- A good way to prepare the people for the pastor's message.
- The time in the meeting to get blessed.
- A good time to bring our prayers to the Lord.

More than anything else, it should be a time where God's people can come before His throne of grace to make known their gratitude to Him and for His Grace, and to proclaim His glory. It is in an attitude of "giving" and not one of "coming to receive" that we should come before Him.

A sacrifice of Thanks Giving

Worship should have only one receptacle: God. Most often, we have an attitude of receiving a blessing from God rather than an attitude of giving back to God.

Let's look at what the apostle Paul says in verses 11 to 14 in chapter 1 of his epistle to the Ephesians: *"In Him we were also chosen, having been predestined according to the plan of Him who works out everything in conformity with the purpose of His will, in order that we, who were the first to hope in Christ, **might be for the praise of His glory**. And you also were included in Christ when you heard the word of truth, the gospel of your salvation. Having believed, you were marked in Him with a seal, the promised Holy Spirit, who is a deposit guaranteeing our inheritance **until the redemption of those who are God's possession – to the praise of His glory.**"*

It is imperative that we remain in this attitude for ministry (one of service) when we worship the Lord. And this is irrespective of what happens during the time of worship: if He speaks, heals, saves someone, Hallelujah!!!

But if it seems to us that nothing is happening, if our souls don't feel His presence, if no prophetic word is brought, rather than thinking that God is not there, remember that this time of praise and worship is addressed to Him, that He promised us His presence where two or three are gathered in His name, and that if He says nothing, it is perhaps because He is just enjoying our worship.

This implies too that we should ask the Holy Spirit to purify our motivation.

Our motivation

Why am I here, why make nice music, why worry about having many good-quality instruments, why have banners, dancing, why displays and paintings…?

If the answer to this is anything other than to draw people to the throne of God, without leaving anyone outside of His courts, or worse still, on the edge of the road to get there, then I am not fulfilling my job as the worship leader.

When I carry out my ministry of "singer" in the meeting, my job is not only to lift my voice up before the Lord, but to do it in such a way that all the people can enter in to meet with God. Sometimes, this is a service that requires a sacrifice, as it may mean we have to be prepared to be in the background a bit, even if we are clearly in view.

We need to understand that the singer must not always be the one to enter first into the Holy of Holies, but rather, should ensure that everyone is able to enter that place.

This notion of service is of prime importance for anyone who wants to serve through praise and worship.

Different aids for worship in the church

In the Word of God, we find several ways of worshipping God. We will try and see what these are and whether they are still in use today. Let us read together from 1 Chronicles 15 and 16: *"So the priests and Levites consecrated themselves in order to bring up the ark of the Lord, the God of Israel."*

One of the first things we notice is that before anything happens, we need to sanctify ourselves and sanctify the aids we use for leading worship. One of my friends, an excellent guitarist, had to leave his guitar in his cupboard for a season, as it was a real idol in his life. It is not possible to be pleasing to God if we come before Him with our idols.

Personally, I believe that all artistic expressions are great for worshipping God, as long as they have been purified in our hearts by the fire of God.

"David told the leaders of the Levites to appoint their brothers as singers." Who are the singers? The first time they are mentioned in the Bible is when the ark is brought up to Jerusalem. It seems that it was David who officially instituted their function (1 Chron 6 vs 32). They were praise and worship "professionals" in the sense that they had this specific full-time ministry.

In fact, they were *"… exempt from other duties because they were responsible for the work day and night."*
(1 Chron 9 vs 33)

To me, it seems urgent that we rediscover the true value of this ministry in the church today! For God is enthroned in the midst of the praises of His people and we are all seeking the presence of God today. That is the calling of the church for eternity.

"… accompanied by musical instruments: lyres, harps and cymbals."

To do this, we see that David had instruments of all sorts given to the singers. The instruments mentioned here were not specifically created for this purpose. They were well-known at that time, used by dancers, "night clubs" of the time (tambourines), just as they were used by the priests in pagan idol worship (cymbals). In other words, what I am trying to say is that there are no good or bad instruments for worship. Nor are there good or bad styles of music.

"… singers who should play loudly on musical instruments…to raise sounds of joy." (RSV)

It is difficult to play the cymbals softly! And I think David knew that, and deliberately chose this instrument to make a loud noise during times of celebration. Psalm 150 vs 5 says, *"Praise Him with the clash of cymbals; praise Him with resounding cymbals!"*.

Seven times in the Psalms, we find the words, *"Shout for joy"*.

During the praise and worship too, there is the right time for everything. A time to let one's joy explode in God's presence, and to join together in this same presence!

"Mattithiah, Eliphelehu, Mikneiah, Obed-Edom, Jeiel and Azaziah were to play the harps, directing according to sheminith." (1 Chro. 15:21)

Singing has an important place in musical worship, as it allows the proclamation of the Word.

It also allows us to express our hearts, *"for out of the overflow of his heart, his mouth speaks"* (Luke 6 vs 45)

One thing is sure, and that is that no-one would have been allowed to clash the cymbals noisily while Azaziah was leading a song!

"Keneniah the head Levite was in charge of the singing; that was his responsibility because he was skilful at it."

God distributes talents to each one so that we may carry out a specific ministry. The same can be said for worship. Even if we ourselves don't qualify in terms of talent, it is Biblical to choose someone who is *"skilful"*, in other words, equipped by God to lead the worship during the meeting!

"… God had helped the Levites who were carrying the ark of the covenant of the Lord…"

Apart from talent, the worship-leader needs to have an anointing to do it. It is with God's help that the worship-leader must lead the people into the courts and right to the throne of grace. It is this anointing, acquired through having personal fellowship with God, that will allow the worship-leader to lead these times.

"…As the ark of the covenant of the Lord was entering the City of David, Michal daughter of Saul watched from a window. And when she saw King David dancing and celebrating, she despised him in her heart."

Sometimes during a meeting, God will appear in a staggering manner. His glory suddenly invades the place. We cannot and, indeed, should not remain stoic when this happens. David allowed himself to be carried away by his ENTHUSIASM.

Do you know that found in the root of this term is the Greek word, "Theos" (God) and translated literally, it means "exalted by the presence of God"?

There is, therefore, nothing negative about being so overcome by His presence that we exult and enthuse! On the contrary! Many Christians need to be a bit more enthusiastic! It is good to dance before God, to jump in His presence, and quite simply, to be enthusiastic!

"They brought the ark of God and set it inside the tent that David had pitched for it, and they presented burnt offerings and fellowship offerings before God."

Our offerings are also a way of worshipping God, which we have seen already. Don't be stingy with the Lord. Let us testify of our confidence in Him with our burnt offerings. That is also a way of worshipping in spirit and in truth. As I have said before, we do not come before our God with empty hands!

After David had finished sacrificing the burnt offerings and fellowship offerings, he blessed the people in the name of the Lord. Then he gave a loaf of bread, a cake of dates and a cake of raisins to each Israelite man and woman…"

(All the previous verses about David worship can be found in the first book of Chronicles)

Fellowship is another way of worshipping the Lord! When we meet to share a meal together, an Agape, which in Greek means "brotherly love", we rejoice God's heart. We are worshipping Him through the testimony of our love for each other.

Relearning how to have a party!

Do you know that at least 36 times in His Word, God orders us to REJOICE? I say "at least" because I have only counted the times when He tells us specifically, "Rejoice". He uses the Hebrew word *"ranan"*, which can be translated literally as: Triumph, come to the end of your difficulties, dominate. Give a loud shout, acclamations of joy.

We absolutely must bring back this festive dimension to our services. God wants His people to be joyful because it is there that we find our strength. The following two texts are pretty convincing:

1 Chron. 16 vs 27: *"Splendour and majesty are before him; strength and joy in his dwelling-place."* When we go into God's dwelling place, the meeting of the brothers, or quite simply, during our own personal time with God, we go into the source of strength and joy.

This joy is to be expected since it comes from meeting with our Father, but sometimes, I hear people saying that since it is spiritual, it should not be expressed in the flesh.

This is an error that still persists today in certain deadly-dull churches. Let us rather read the other passage that speaks about this issue of joy and strength.

Nehemiah 8 vs 10: *"Nehemiah said, 'Go and enjoy choice food and sweet drinks, and send some to those who have nothing prepared. This day is sacred to our Lord. Do not grieve, for the joy of the Lord is your strength."*

Dear friends, fatty meat and sweet liqueurs are not exactly spiritual fare, but are certainly pleasures belonging to the flesh. God asks His people to have a party in order to remind themselves of all the important steps in their history and in their relationship with Him (Passover, bread without yeast, tabernacles, harvest…). We who celebrate the resurrection of Christ, do we not have good reason to rejoice?

Too many Christians rejoice more easily when their favourite soccer team wins a match than when it comes to celebrating the King of Kings!! Is this how it should really be?

Learning again how to proclaim:

It is imperative that we understand the importance of proclaiming the Word during our time of worship.

Let's read together from Genesis 1: *"And God said, 'Let there be light,' and there was light… And God said, 'Let there be an expanse between the waters to separate water from water'… And it was so."*

Every word that God pronounces has creative force and does not remain without effect.
(See Josh 23 vs 14). In the same way, our words can also have creative power when they are inspired by the Holy Spirit or by the Word of God.

When I worship God in proclaiming that He is the Eternal One who heals, who provides, etc, I am giving Him the possibility to manifest these things in the midst of His people. By proclaiming what we have learnt about God's promises in His word, we put substance onto our faith.

A wonderful example of this is found in the book of Chronicles in the story of Jehoshaphat. Let's look at 2 Chronicles 20: *"After this, the Moabites and the Ammonites with some of the Meunites came to make war on Jehoshaphat…" In his fear, Jehoshaphat sought the Lord. …'Oh Lord, God of our fathers, are you not the God who is in heaven? You rule over all the kingdoms of the nations…' All the men of Judah with their wives and their children and little ones, stood there before the Lord. Then the Spirit of the Lord came upon Jahaziel… He said, 'Listen, King Jehoshaphat and all who live in Judah and Jerusalem! This is what the Lord says to you: Do not be afraid or discouraged because of this vast army. For the battle is not yours, but God's. Tomorrow march down against them… You will not have to fight this battle. Take up your positions; stand firm and see the deliverance the Lord will give you…'*

Early in the morning, they left for the Desert of Tekoa. As they set out, Jehoshaphat stood and said, 'Listen to me, Judah and people of Jerusalem! Have faith in the Lord your God'… After consulting the people, Jehoshaphat appointed men to march ahead of the army, celebrating the Lord! As they began to sing and praise, the Lord set ambushes against the men of Ammon and Moab and Mount Seir who were invading Judah, and they were defeated… When the men of Judah came to the place that overlooks the desert and looked towards the vast army, they saw only dead bodies lying on the ground… and they found among them a great amount of equipment and clothing and also articles of value

– more than they could take away. There was so much plunder that it took three days to collect it."

In this passage, we get an understanding of what it means to proclaim. It is not just a simple word that we tirelessly keep repeating. That would be more like a "mantra" or positive thinking, which are pale, pathetic copies of a proclamation of faith. In actual fact, this is about our proclaiming as much in word as in action that the Lord is God.

Jehoshaphat understood this. He received the prophetic word from Jahaziel saying that God would fight in their place, and in turn, he proclaimed it with his mouth. But importantly, he acted as a result of this proclamation and against all strategic logic: he sent the singers in the front line, because he knew, he had the faith, that he would not have to fight, for God would do it in their place.

God speaks, Jehoshaphat proclaims that word and he carries out the action in faith! It is in this way that promises can be fulfilled. Proclaiming a promise is claiming it through faith. The Word of God is full of treasures that we need to make our own, thanking God through worship for these promises. For a promise is reality for those who claim it with faith. The Word of God must not be far away from our hearts; thus, our hearts will become full of this marvellous treasure.

"The good man brings good things out of the good stored up in his heart, and the evil man brings evil things out of

the evil stored up in his heart. For out of the overflow of his heart his mouth speaks."
(Luke 6 vs 45)

Prophetic worship

The conclusion we can draw from reading those passages in Chronicles brings us to realise that worship, in the time of David, was a real source of the prophetic.

I have always been amazed when reading a psalm like Psalm 22. Jesus and Calvary is described with such precision… completely "prophetically". Even the words of Christ, *"My God! My God! Why have you forsaken me…"* The supplication from the cross is described here even though in the time of David, He was unknown in the Middle East!

This is but one example among so many others in Biblical passages. We can explain this in two ways.

Firstly, when we proclaim the reign of Christ in our worship, His power, His return, etc, we are proclaiming something prophetic: the fulfilment is not yet visible, but we affirm it because we have faith in what the Spirit of God is inspiring in us.

Secondly, our worship is prophetic because it attracts God's presence: *"Yet you are holy; you are enthroned on the praises of Israel."* (Psalm 22 vs 3). This presence is the source of the prophetic.

Often, after a time of worship, the Spirit inspires in me a worship song or a prophetic proclamation. I am able to describe through song a vision that I see in the spirit. Often, I am unable to repeat what I have sung, or the chords I have played, at the end of the service.

We need to be attentive to the prophetic Spirit when we are leading praise and worship in order not to stifle Him. During a time of worship, there is nothing worse than starting up a song to fill the silence where God wants to speak.

Let us remember that we are there for Him. He must be the centre of our attention; we must, therefore, ensure that He is the one who is the centre and is leading our worship. If we do, our worship will become truly prophetic.

To conclude this chapter, I simply want to point out the splendour of worship during the time of David. We consciously need to allow this kind of worship to return to our meetings today, since, *"The law is only a shadow of the good things that are coming – not the realities themselves. For this reason, it can never, by the same sacrifices repeated endlessly year after year, make perfect those who draw near to worship."* (Hebrews 10 vs 1)

We need to go right to the end of this process.

"Yet a time is coming and has now come when the true worshippers will worship the Father in spirit and in truth,

for they are the kind of worshippers the Father seeks." (John 4 vs 23)

Real worship, it seems to me, is the ultimate end result of our praise and worship. It is the moment when we abandon ourselves completely in the hands of God. It is at this moment that we can be worshippers in spirit and in truth. Whereas the festive side of praise, or again, the proclamation of faith can be, to some extent, "positively flesh-filled", real worship of God is purely spiritual.

This is why our true worship is something that has to come from our heart, rather than our lips.

If our declarations, as we have already seen, are important because of the power that they result in, what counts to God is not that we tell Him that He is a great God, but that we act as a result of it.

Nothing is gained by declaring that He is great if I am not able to trust Him in all areas of my life.

He does not expect us to be perfect before He will accept our worship. That is, after all, why Jesus went before us into the Holy of Holies, through His own blood, so that we might have access to the Father. But God wants us to abandon ourselves completely to Him.

BUILDING THE TEMPLE

Now I would like to come back to the notion of the tabernacle of David, which is something the church seems to have rediscovered over the past few years. Many consider this to be a fad that is in fashion and frankly, they are not entirely wrong.

In fact, the Holy Spirit has accelerated a process of restoration in the church which began even before the Reformation in the 17th century, with the consort of Jean Hus and Pierre Valdo.

This process brought the church to place of gradually rediscovering the most important points of Biblical teaching that had been forgotten.

Luther rediscovered salvation through grace, the Anabaptists adult baptism for converted adults, the Methodists the necessity of evangelism which ran counter to the Calvinist doctrine at that time, the Pentecostals speaking in tongues and the gifts of the Holy Spirit … Since the beginning of the 20th century, this tendency has been accelerating and every 10 to 15 years, a new church movement is born.

If each of these rediscoveries is a wonderful thing in itself, wanting to separate itself from what preceded it - just as new movements to come will do - is complete folly!

In each wave of the Spirit, many people think this is now THE Revival. They often despise the foundations of the previous revival on which their revival has been built, and they passionately refute the awakening that follows their one.

This is how, from one revival to another, we see the persecuted of yesterday becoming the persecutors of today, believing that the revelation they received is THE final revelation. They usually believe that if there is to be another revelation, it will obviously come to them, seeing as they were the ones who were led to receive the previous revelation!

For my part, I believe there is a real danger of immobility, even if I myself organise praise and worship sessions lasting several hours and I consider that the "Tabernacle of David" is not an end in itself. I particularly love worship, music when it is anointed by God, teams of singers who work hard to offer up to God the best of themselves. But all of this will come to an end one day, in order to make place for something greater still.

David, who set up his Tabernacle, had another goal in mind: that of building a temple to the Lord.

Let's read together some verses from chapter 17 in the first book of Chronicles, verses 1 to 4:

"After David was settled in his palace, he said to Nathan the prophet, 'Here I am, living in a palace of cedar, while the ark of the covenant of the Lord is under a tent.'

Nathan replied to David, 'Whatever you have in mind, do it, for God is with you.'

That night the word of God came to Nathan, saying: 'Go and tell my servant David: This is what the Lord says: You are not the one to build me a house to dwell in.'".

We have looked at the splendour of continuous praise and worship organised under the Tabernacle of David together. But this was not an end in itself. David wanted to build a wonderful, grandiose temple to the glory of God!

Of course, some people find it puerile that David could even think he would be able to offer God a place where He would live. The Creator of the universe, who is seated in the heavens and whose stepping stones are the earth, how is it possible to build a temple worthy of His glory?

Others may think that this idea was the fruit of pride on David's part and that this was why God would not allow him to build this temple.

Others might say that it was to prevent the people from falling back into the old mistake of wanting to turn God into something material (like the golden calf) and that building the temple would have allowed the people to crystallise their faith into something concrete.

But whatever reason it was that pushed David to embark on this project, I think the most interesting thing was the answer God gave to His servant. Whilst David wanted to build a house for the eternal God, actually God Himself declared He would build a house for David (verses 10 to 14): *"…'"I declare to you that the Lord will build a house for you: When your days are over and you go to be with your fathers, I will raise up your offspring to succeed you, one of your own sons, and I will establish his kingdom. He is the one who will build a house for me, and I will establish his throne for ever. I will be his father, and he will be my son. I will never take my love away from him, as I took it away from your predecessor. I will set him over my house and my kingdom for ever; his throne will be established for ever.'"*

It is easy for us to understand which descendant this is about! Our Lord Jesus. The Lord explains His perfect plan to David in a few words, giving a meaning to the future words of Christ.

God's plan is not that we build a temple for Him. *"He is the one who will build a house for me, and I will establish his throne for ever."* This prophetic word would be announced again by Jesus Himself in John 2 vs 19 : *"Jesus replied to them, 'Destroy this temple, and I will raise it again in three days.'"*

We can all understand that Jesus was not speaking there of the temple of stones built by Herod, but of the temple that was Jesus Himself.

In Matthew 16 vs 18, He explains how He Himself would rebuild the temple that God had spoken of in the passage in Chronicles: *"And I tell you that you are Peter, and on this rock I will build my church."* In fact, it is Peter's declaration, *"You are the Messiah"*, which is the rock upon which Jesus would build His church. In other words, the fact that Jesus was announced as the messiah, gave Him the legitimate right to build this temple that God had promised to David.

The first stone of this building would be placed in position at the time of the ascension:
Acts 1 vs 4 – 8: *"On one occasion while he was eating with them, he gave them this command: 'Do not leave Jerusalem, but wait for the gift my Father promised, which you have heard me speak about. For John baptised with water, but in a few days, you will be baptised with the Holy Spirit.' So when they met together, they asked him, 'Lord, are you at this time going to restore the kingdom to Israel?' He said to them, 'It is not for you to know the times or dates the Father has set by his own authority. But you will receive power when the Holy Spirit comes on you; and you will be my witnesses in Jerusalem, and in all Judea and Samaria, and to the ends of the earth."*

What is the church?

I personally believe the best definition of what the church is can be found in the following verses:
"As you come to Him, the living Stone – rejected by men but chosen by God and precious to Him – you also, like

living stones, are being built into a spiritual house to be a holy priesthood, offering spiritual sacrifices acceptable to God through Jesus Christ." (1 Peter 2 vs 4 and 5).

If we want to build a temple of worship to our God, it is imperative that we build it with living stones.

The question we need to ask ourselves, before building it, is: "Are we living stones or tomb stones?"

Sometimes, I wonder if Jesus would declare about me what He said in Matthew 23 vs 27:

"Woe to you, teachers of the law and Pharisees, you hypocrites! You are like whitewashed tombs, which look beautiful on the outside but on the inside are full of dead men's bones and everything unclean."

We lift our hands high in church; we shout "Hallelujah" and "Amen" loudly; we give our tithes and offerings and all these things are good. But what goes on after the service when we go home? Are we still so alive and zealous? In our daily lives, do we have the same enthusiasm to call ourselves alive Christians?

For many Christians, the principles of life in Christ seem to be incompatible with daily reality. At the end of the day, many only seem to be alive on a Sunday morning between nine o'clock and midday, then they die from Monday onwards until the following Sunday, when they are resurrected again.

These are not the kind of stones we can use to build a glorious temple!

We need to understand as well that in building this temple to the glory of God, Jesus does not use bricks that all look like each other, but living stones.

Have you ever seen two identical stones in nature? Of course not! Each one is different, and that's what makes God's creation so beautiful! When we build something using natural stones, we don't plaster over it, as that would mask the beauty of the stones!

We only use plaster if we are building with blocks that are all the same, which are easy to lay on top of each other, but not particularly beautiful!

It is the same with the church when it is built using Christians, "living stones": it is much more difficult to construct. There is more work required, because one needs to find which stone will work well with which. Time is needed to clean the stones so that they can be used in such a way for the best to be brought out in each of them. One needs to lay each one carefully according its uniqueness, not just according to how the stone itself looks, but looking ahead to how it will be part of the whole. When all this work has been done, our wall is a wonder to see because of the beauty of the stones. It becomes a work of art. The Church, Christ's fiancée, is worthy of her King!

If, however, one constructs it with "block" Christians, all the same, the building goes more quickly, but one has to apply plaster onto it … religiosity! Too many pastors want to build too quickly, even if it means breaking the life of the living stones entrusted to them by God in their "brick mould".

If you speak of living stones, then you are speaking of stones that change constantly! Every Christian, if he is alive, is a ministry in progress. Let us allow each one the time to become the stone that God wants to make him into! It is He who will cut and shape, who will choose the exact place where the stone will be placed in order to be best anchored with the others and where it will have the best effect! God, who knows exactly the final goal that He is wanting to attain, does not see us as the stones we are today, but as stones once they have been cleaned, shaped, put together with others.

We often do things differently when it comes to how we build. We prefer to have bricks that are ready to use. We often demand Christians who fit into the template of our plan. If they don't conform to that, we reject them, convinced that even God Himself will not be able to do anything with them. This, alas, is also true of some of God's servants who have not understood that their role in the building of this temple is not to be the architect, but the Lord's labourer!

How does Christ build His church?

I believe that today, we are in the final phase of this building. For some years already, the church has rediscovered the reality of the five-fold ministry and has accepted that this needs to be manifested in these days, after centuries during which the five-fold ministry stayed in a kind of "hibernation".

But let us look again at God's intended purpose for these five ministries.

"It was he who gave some to be apostles, some to be prophets, some to be evangelists, and some to be pastors and teachers, to prepare God's people for works of service, so that the body of Christ may be built up until we all reach unity in the faith and in the knowledge of the Son of God and become mature, attaining to the whole measure of the fullness of Christ." (Ephesians 4 vs 11 to 13)

Some people still believe today that the ministry of apostles, prophets etc disappeared when the Bible was compiled, with the Bible being what brings the Body of Christ to unity in the faith.

But we should surely realise that up to now, this unity is still far from being established. We will, therefore, see the five-fold ministry at work, *"until we all reach unity in the faith"!*

Unity in the faith does not at all mean that we all have to agree on everything. Many people believe that the fact that they are right automatically implies that the others are wrong, and this is false!

God alone has an overview of what faith is, and it is time that we admit it. We will only have perfect knowledge of His works and His word when we are raised up to meet Him. In the meantime, in His wisdom, He shared out this knowledge between the different great trends of Christianity. He has done this to force us to work together in order for us to be at our most effective in His great work.

Some people consider it demonic that there are so many different denominations and churches. I, on the other hand, consider it to be the fruit of the wisdom of God.

Unity in the faith is understanding that, whatever our differences, we are called to be united with all other Christians. Not through our doctrines, but by the grace that God showed towards us in sending us His Son! If this is not yet the case, it is what we should be aiming at. How many Bible verses are there that command us to walk in love and unity!

We need to understand that there can be no praise and worship enjoyed by God when there is division and contempt towards the rest of the Body of Christ.

This principle is revealed to us in taking Communion, an act of worship *par excellence* as the apostle Paul describes it to us in 1 Cor 11 vs 27 to 31: *"Therefore, whoever eats the bread or drinks the cup of the Lord in an unworthy manner will be guilty of sinning against the body and blood of the Lord. A man ought to examine himself before he eats of the bread and drinks of the cup. For whoever eats and drinks without recognising the body of the Lord, eats and drinks judgment upon himself. That is why many among you are weak and sick and a number of you have fallen asleep. But if we judged ourselves, we would not come under judgment."*

3) What does "whoever eats the bread or drinks the cup of the Lord in an unworthy manner" mean?

The purpose of Communion is to remember the most important thing that happened during Jesus' time on earth. That thing is neither one of His teachings, nor a miracle that happened. It is the redemptive sacrifice that He accomplished for us, for all who believe in Him, and it is free.

Paul warns us, therefore, of the danger of despising those to whom this salvation is for, whilst we ourselves are beneficiaries of it.

He specifically says in the next bit of this passage, *"For whoever eats and drinks without recognising the body of the Lord, eats and drinks judgment upon himself."*

Now the body of the Lord is made up of all those who have believed! Without exception!

Paul declares here that if there are sick people and even some deaths, it is because some believe themselves more capable than God Himself of discerning who is, or is not, part of the body of Christ. Paul reminds us here of the story of the speck and the log. *"If we judged ourselves, we would not be judged!"*

Remember that the context of this letter that Paul is sending to the Corinthians is division. To convince ourselves of this fact, let's read how Paul begins his letter: Paul begins his greeting by explaining that we are all saved by our faith in Jesus Christ and that this implies we belong to Him and that from now on, we are called to live FOR HIM!: *"I am writing to God's church in Corinth, to you who have been called by God to be his own holy people. He made you holy by means of Jesus Christ…"* (NLT).

He continues his greeting by giving his blessing to all those who believe in Christ, whatever local body they are part of, declaring that their Lord and his are one and the same!
"…just as he did for all people everywhere who call on the name of our Lord Jesus Christ, their Lord and ours. May God our Father and the Lord Jesus Christ give you grace and peace." (NLT)

Paul then goes on with the following urgent appeal: *"I appeal to you, brothers, in the name of our Lord Jesus Christ, that all of you agree with one another so that there may be no divisions among you and that you may be perfectly united in mind and thought."*

He declares that our goal should be, above everything else, to belong to the body of Christ, and in no case, to a specific denomination: *"What I mean is this: One of you says, 'I follow Paul'; another, 'I follow Apollos'; another, 'I follow Peter; still another, ;'I follow Christ.'"*

He clearly says that the body of Christ cannot be divided! *"Is Christ divided? Was Paul crucified for you? Were you baptised in the name of Paul?"*

So often, we spend more time endlessly discussing other people's errors rather than testifying the love and the respect that we ought to show them as brothers in Christ.

Isaiah 58 vs 9 and 10 tell us: *"Then you will call, and the Lord will answer; you will cry for help, and he will say: 'Here am I.' If you do away with the yoke of oppression, with the pointing finger and malicious talk, and if you spend yourselves on behalf of the hungry and satisfy the needs of the oppressed, then your light will rise in the darkness, and your night will become like the noonday."*

God does not want us to mock and speak maliciously. Rather, He wants us to be witnesses of His love, as much in how we speak as in our actions. Then our night will be lit up as the noonday.

How often, my friends, have we lost this perspective? How often have we missed the mark (which is actually the definition of the word "sin") in striving to point out the faults in everything that moves away from our limited understanding of the plan? How often have we forgotten to love?

I am not trying to be alarmist, but simply to be lucid. We need to confess our sins to God because this is what it is about, and we need to ask Him to change our way of thinking.

Our hearts do not have the capacity to love God as we ought. Loving our enemies, those who annoy us, those who persecute us, those who don't have the same doctrine as we do etc. This is not something that can be done in our souls, but in our spirits. And we need to realise that not one of us can produce any fruit of the Spirit from our souls!

How, then, can we have Christ's feelings for our neighbour? How do we live out the commandment *"Love one another"* in our daily lives?

Christ managed because He was not "DOCTRINE-CENTRED"!

Sometimes, it seems to me, and maybe it happens to you too, that I am no better than the Pharisees who criticised Jesus for healing on the Sabbath.

We think of ourselves as the valiant defenders of holy doctrine and we speak of theological purity, forgetting that the logic of Theo - God - is LOVE, which surpasses everything else.

For this Love to become a reality, we need to learn how to consider others as being as important, if not more so, than ourselves in God's plan. This becomes possible if we keep our eyes fixed on Jesus more than on ourselves.

When John describes the worship happening before the throne of God, he does so in these terms:

"Each of the four living creatures had six wings and was covered with eyes all around, even under his wings. Day and night, they never stop saying:

'Holy, holy, holy is the Lord God Almighty, who was, and is, and is to come.'

Whenever the living creatures give glory, honour and thanks to him who sits on the throne and who lives for ever and ever, the twenty-four elders fall down before him who sits on the throne, and worship him who lives for ever and ever. They lay their crowns before the throne and say:

'You are worthy, our Lord and God, to receive glory and honour and power, for you created all things, and by your will they were created and have their being.'" (Revelation 4 vs 8 – 11)

We, too, need to be prepared to cast down our crowns at the feet of Christ. The crown of our position in the local church, of our successes, even of our ministry.

I am convinced that if we did not attach as much importance to all of these things, we would be on far better terms with other people and with God too!

Our crowns have become idols. They have taken the place that belongs to God in our worship as soon as they become more important in our eyes than the brother or sister who is standing next to us! And this is so often the case! And how about our brothers and sisters in other churches or church groups!?

The temple, which is the body of Christ, does not have only one wall, but several walls, doors, watchtowers etc. This is how it becomes a fortress in whose shadow we can shelter. A single wall has never managed to stop an enemy army. Quite simply because anyone can get behind a single wall! In the Second World War, the French learnt this the hard way with the Maginot Line!

Even if our church is built with beautiful living stones, but stays isolated in its own corner, it will be like a wall planted in the middle of a field! To begin with, it will be a weak wall, as nothing is supporting it at each end, but more than that, it will be a useless wall! The whole point of building walls is to construct a building in which one can find shelter. A single wall is not a shelter and cannot protect anyone! By necessity, several walls are required.

God planned for his temple to be built with several walls that would thus create a fortress of worship and prayer in the face of our enemies! Luke 19 verse 46: *"My house will be a house of prayer."*

4) One people, 12 Tribes… clans and families!

The way that God structured the people of Israel is rich in teachings for those who want to understand the diversity of the different churches we find in the body of Christ today.

The Bible explains to us that the people of Israel were divided into twelve tribes, which were then divided into clans which, in turn, were divided into families. Judges 6:15 says "*But Lord," Gideon asked, "how can I save Israel? My clan is the weakest in Manasseh, and I am the least in my family.*"

We need to understand that the fact of belonging to the smallest family did not exclude from the family of God as a whole. On the contrary! Remember how if a man was a victim of an injustice, they would gather 11 tribes in order for justice to be done for him; and how those 11 tribes would do everything possible to save that 12th tribe threatened with extinction! (Judges 19 to 21).

Sometimes we forget that the only two rules that sealed the relationship between the twelve tribes of Israel were:

1. Praise: all the people were expected to go to Jerusalem, to a single place, in order to worship God. Although in today's world, we no longer gather in a single place, the unity in spirit in praise and worship remains the same.

2. Warfare: in times of conflict, every tribe was expected to offer assistance to the others. Sadly, what we more often seem to do is to take pleasure in attacks that come against

"competing churches" instead of standing by them and helping in times of trouble! Some even go so far as to "intercede" (sic) for the downfall of another church group!

If God decided it was a good idea to give us an example to follow in this "school of how to do church", which is what Israel's life in the Old Testament represents, it seems incongruous to me to declare that different denominations are the work of the devil. What *is* the work of Satan is when we elevate one denomination over another.

If we want to be part of His plan, it is imperative that we understand that this cannot happen without the other members of the body of Christ. It is only when we do it together that God accepts the praises that we lift up to Him. And He feels likewise concerning everything to do with establishing His Kingdom.

A few years ago, I received this word: *"I am seeking a people who are road-builders and bridge-makers,",* says the Lord, *"not wall-builders."* Our problem is that we are the ones who are trying to build the church, instead of allowing Christ to do it. And often, we build impenetrable fortresses suited more to other Christians than to the lost! Whereas God asks us to build roads that lead to Christ and doors that provide access to the Lord's temple!

It is high time we understand that we are not called to fill our churches, but to empty hell!

Often, we lose the perspective that belonging to a local church is not only good in itself, but necessary. The local church is the place for us to grow, learn, receive the call of God on our lives. We owe loyalty and love to our local church, but that doesn't necessarily mean we have to spend our whole lives there. There are seasons in which we need to learn how to change pastures!

WHEN THE CLOUD OF GOD COMES TO DWELL AMONG US!

This is where we see the famous revival that each of us is aspiring to. The cloud of God that covers everything and in which the enemy cannot bear to be. We have experienced this occasionally, but God wants this to be a daily reality in our meetings, as He never intended it to be anything else for His church. Remember Mark 16: *"And these signs will accompany those who believe…"*

We often sing, "Not by might, nor by power, but by your Spirit…" The Holy Spirit dwells in the midst of a temple of praise to our God! It is when the cloud comes to rest among us that we can really know it is God leading His people.

But do we know exactly what that cloud is? We can be sure that it is there from the beginning to the end of the Word of God. The cloud is often related to the glorious presence of God, which the Israelites called *"Shekinah"*.

There are several passages in Scripture that mention this presence:

2 Chronicles 5 vs 11-14: *"The priests then withdrew from the Holy Place. All the priests who were there had consecrated themselves, regardless of their divisions. All the Levites who were musicians – Asaph, Heman, Jeduthun and their sons and relatives – stood on the east side of the altar, dressed in fine linen and playing cymbals, harps and lyres. They were accompanied by 120 priests sounding trumpets. The trumpeters and singers joined in unison, as with one voice, to give praise and thanks to the Lord. Accompanied by trumpets, cymbals, and other instruments, they raised their voices in praise to the Lord and sang: 'He is good; his love endures for ever.' Then the temple of the Lord was filled with a cloud, and the priests could not perform their service because of the cloud, for the glory of the Lord filled the temple of God."*

Ezekiel 10 vs 4: *"… Then the glory of the Lord rose from above the cherubim and moved to the threshold of the temple. The cloud filled the temple, and the court was full of the radiance of the glory of the Lord."*

Luke 21 vs 27: *"At that time they will see the Son of Man coming in a cloud with power and great glory."*

However, we cannot limit this cloud as the only sign of God's presence! God is present in the midst of us and that should have immediate consequences, not only on our "being", but also on our "actions". It comes back, then, to understanding the different roles that the cloud has had in the Bible and up to this day. It is a role that should still be active in the present day and in our lives.

Let us study what this cloud does in the Old and New Testaments.

1. The cloud serves as a guide!

Exodus 13 vs 21: *"By day the Lord went ahead of them in a pillar of cloud to guide them on their way and by night in a pillar of fire to give them light, so that they could travel by day or night."*

In this passage, we see that the role of the cloud is to guide Israel in their walk in the desert. We know that God's people moved camps whenever the cloud moved. When it stopped, they set up the tent of meeting at that very spot, and they did not move on until the cloud moved.

Numbers 9 vs 7 – 19: *"Whenever the cloud lifted from above the Tent, the Israelites set out; wherever the cloud settled, the Israelites encamped. At the Lord's command, the Israelites set out, and at his command, they encamped. As long as the cloud rested over the tabernacle, they remained in camp. When the cloud rested over the tabernacle for a long time, the Israelites obeyed the Lord's order and did not set out."*

The people obeyed the commands of the cloud, just as Jesus and the Apostles of the New Testament submitted themselves to the Holy Spirit in terms of their movements.

Luke 4 vs 1: *"Jesus, full of the Holy Spirit, returned from the Jordan and was led by the Spirit in the desert."*

Acts 13 vs 4: *"The two of them [Barnabas and Saul], sent on their way by the Holy Spirit, went down to Seleucia and sailed from there to Cyprus."*

Acts 16 vs 6: *"Paul and his companions travelled throughout the regions of Phrygia and Galatia, having been kept by the Holy Spirit from preaching the word in the province of Asia."*

Acts 20 vs 22: *"And now, compelled by the Spirit, I am going to Jerusalem…"*

2. The cloud protects!

Exodus 14 vs 19-20, 24: *"The angel of God, who had been travelling in front of Israel's army, withdrew and went behind them. The pillar of cloud also moved from in front and stood behind them, coming between the armies of Egypt and Israel. Throughout the night the cloud brought darkness to the one side and light to the other side; so neither went near the other all night long… In the morning watch the Lord looked down from the pillar of fire and cloud at the Egyptian army and threw it into confusion."*

If we are faithful in allowing the Spirit/the cloud of God to lead us, we live under His protection as Israel did during its escape from Egypt.

Sometimes it may seem to us that the directives of this cloud are not very judicious and that His choices are questionable. Pharaoh must surely have mocked Moses and his God who were very poor strategists to trap the people in a cul-de-sac like this one. But it always turns out that God knows what He is doing, and in the most perilous situations, He is always there, in that cloud, to protect us. Hallelujah!

3. The cloud anoints with authority and power!

Matthew 17 vs 5: *"While He was still speaking, a bright cloud enveloped them, and a voice from the cloud said, 'This is my Son, whom I love; with him I am well pleased. Listen to him!'"*

Many people seek authority in the world - one that will allow them to be recognised by those like themselves. This authority generally rests on their ability to lead or sometimes, on their skills, and sometimes even, simply because they were born "on the right side of the tracks"!

But God works differently. Remember how He chose a replacement for King Saul. David's authority was not based on his abilities, but on the fact that he had received the royal anointing from Samuel!

In the same way, Jesus proclaims that His authority comes from this anointing: Luke 4 vs 8:

The Spirit of the Lord is upon me because he has anointed me…"

Jesus bases His authority on this fact: He has been anointed by God! From which comes the name of Christ, which means, *"anointed"*.

Obviously, this authority, just as happened with David, would be contested. Therefore, why would the world, that refuses to recognise the authority of our God, recognise the authority of those He sent to it?

Acts 4 vs 26 and 27: *"The kings of the earth take their stand and the rulers gather together against the Lord and against His Anointed One. Indeed, Herod and Pontius Pilate met together with the Gentiles and the people of Israel in this city to conspire against your holy servant Jesus, whom you anointed."*

But recognition by men is of no importance if God recognises you as He recognised Christ:
"You know how God anointed Jesus of Nazareth with the Holy spirit and power, and how he went around doing good and healing all who were under the power of the evil, because God was with him. (Acts 10 vs 38)

4. Receiving the cloud!

1 Cor 10 vs 1 and 2: *"For I do not want you to be ignorant of the fact, brothers, that our forefathers were all under the cloud and that they all passed through the sea. They were all baptised into Moses in the cloud and in the sea."*

In reading this text, it would be difficult not to liken baptism in water and baptism in the Holy Spirit.

Jesus ordered us to receive this cloud/Spirit who would lead us into truth, would comfort us, make us into children of God, but would also equip us to enter into His plan:

Acts 1 vs 8: *"But you will receive power when the Holy Spirit comes on you; and you will be my witnesses in Jerusalem, and in all Judea and Samaria, and to the ends of the earth."*

In order to receive this cloud, we need to seek after it. This is a permanent principle of the Word. "Seek and you will find." "Desire the gifts", etc. Between the Ascension and Pentecost, when the cloud descended upon them, the disciples were in a position of waiting and in prayer for the cloud to descend.

5. It can leave us!

Numbers 12 vs 9 and 10: *"The anger of the Lord burned against them, and he left them. When the cloud lifted from above the Tent, there stood Miriam – leprous, like snow. Aaron turned towards her and saw that she had leprosy."*

We need to understand very clearly that the fact that the cloud rests among us for a time does not mean that we are in the cloud on a permanent basis. Take Saul, who received the anointing and then it was removed afterwards. Later on, the "SHEKINAH" left the Temple, which was subsequently destroyed (2 Kings 25).

6. God is holy; that means His cloud is as well!

Leviticus 16 vs 2: *"The Lord said to Moses: 'Tell your brother Aaron not to come whenever he chooses into the Most Holy Place behind the curtain in front of the atonement cover on the ark, or else he will die, because I appear in the cloud over the atonement cover.'"*

The only chance we may have of staying alive in His cloud is by being sanctified through Jesus. But that does not absolve us from continuing to seek this holiness. We need to think carefully about this so that what happened to Ananias and Saphira is not repeated.

In the New Testament, we see that the Spirit of God can be grieved and will withdraw.
Ephesians 4 vs 30: *"And do not grieve the Holy Spirit of God, with whom you were sealed for the day of redemption."*

The cloud, which we can also call "the anointing" is, at the end of the day, quite simply the presence of God – THE HOLY SPIRIT.

Just as the Father is enthroned in the heavens, Jesus intercedes night and day before His face, and the Holy Spirit, as He promised us, is with us, shown in a very real way through the manifestations of the Anointing.

Just as in Solomon's time when the cloud rested in the temple, we need to seek for the Holy Spirit to rest in the temple that we ourselves have become. In order for this to happen, we need first of all to be sanctified by putting ourselves under the precious blood of Jesus. Then we need to guard against making it unclean again, and to do that, we have to come back to the source of this grace, who is Jesus. So we need to allow this grace to move in us: to allow it - Him - to guide us, to protect us and equip us in order for us to enter into God's perfect plan. Amen.

DEEPER IN THE RIVER

From the spring to the river!

To introduce the next section, we are going to look at two passages in which Jesus refers to the image of running water to illustrate His sermon. But as you will discover, something important changes. Let's read these passages together.

John 4 vs 24 to 14: *"Are you greater than our father Jacob, who gave us the well and drank from it himself, as did also his sons and his flocks and herds?' Jesus answered, 'Everyone who drinks this water will be thirsty again, but whoever drinks the water I give him will never thirst. Indeed, the water I give him will become in him a spring of water welling up to eternal life.'"*

In this first passage, we see Jesus talking to a Samaritan woman. What is He talking about to her? Salvation! That the person who is thirsty should come and drink at the well of Salvation.
Titus 2 vs 11: *"For the grace of God that brings salvation has appeared to all men."*

In the second passage that we are going to read, Jesus no longer alludes to a well, but to a river.
John 7 vs 37 – 39: *"On the last and greatest day of the Feast, Jesus stood and said in a loud voice, 'If any man is thirsty, let him come to me and drink. Whoever believes in me, as the Scripture has said, streams of living water will*

flow from within him.' By this He meant the Spirit, whom those who believed in Him were later to receive. Up to that time the Spirit had not been given, since Jesus had not yet been glorified."

Everyone knows the difference between a well and a river, and I am convinced that if Jesus used the two terms, it was deliberate, because He has something to teach us through it.

We see that Jesus is speaking of a river, alluding to the Holy Spirit. So we need to go…

Deeper in the river!

"He then brought me out through the north gate and led me round the outside to the outer gate facing east, and the water was flowing from the south side. As the man went eastward with a measuring-line in his hand, he measured off a thousand cubits and led me through water that was knee-deep. He measured off another thousand and led me through water that was up to the waist. He measured off another thousand, but now it was a river that I could not cross, because the water had risen and was deep enough to swim in – a river that no-one could cross." (Ezekiel 47 vs 2 – 5)

This vision of Ezekiel is considered to be representative of the Spirit of God. In this passage, we see two things.

The first is that the Spirit of God is so huge that a man, even one filled with the Spirit as Ezekiel was, cannot apprehend Him in His greatness. Before losing his foothold, the prophet would have covered 4000 cubits, which is in the region of 2000 metres.

The second thing revealed to us in the passage is that once he reached that place, the current was so strong that the servant of God lost his foothold and was not able to resist it.

When I read this passage, I can't help realising, for myself, as for a great number of my contemporaries, that we just splash around in a few centimetres of water on the edge of the river of the Spirit. And then we consider ourselves to be more spiritual than others who are not charismatic, who stay right on the banks. But in reality, we are still very far from the degree that God wants us to enter into.

I am becoming more and more convinced that God wants to lead us into things that are completely crazy to us, but oh, how wise to Him! But for this to happen, our reasoning has to fall away. We have to lose our foothold completely, humanly speaking, to be submerged by His Spirit, if we want Him to work through us.

It is from that point that we should expect to see things that will unavoidably shock our powers of reasoning. To some people, it seems ridiculous that we speak in tongues; to others, that people start laughing in the Holy Spirit, fall over because of the Holy Spirit, dance or do many other things because of the Holy Spirit. But is this crazier than saying that Jesus, crucified two thousand years ago, is alive today, or to ask a paralysed person to get up in the Name of Jesus, or even just to accept that God's justice allows the worst of us to be forgiven because He gave His only Son as a sacrifice for the forgiveness of sins?

What prevents us from entering in fully?

There are different reactions towards the Holy Spirit.

Those who stay on dry sand.

These are people who never "get wet". I remember a brother who did not want to tell his friends that he was a Christian, as he was afraid that his friends would not visit him anymore if he took a radical stand.

Other people position themselves in such a way that they belong to a church, but they refuse to allow it to have the slightest implication when it comes to their everyday lives.

Others are very pious, as long as it all stays within acceptable bounds for all, whatever their beliefs or opinions.

The trouble is the Gospel is not there to make peace between us and the world; on the contrary.

John 5 vs 20 – 21 warns us: *"Remember the words I spoke to you: "No servant is greater than his master.' If they persecuted me, they will persecute you also. If they obeyed my teaching, they will obey yours also. They will treat you this way because of my name, for they do not know the One who sent me."*

Those who paddle in 10cm of water.

To do this, all that is required is to remove one's shoes. Here, I see people who refuse to get undressed, most often because of pride, in other words they don't want to lose their image (standing, position in society etc). What will people say if I start saying things that don't make sense. They'll think I'm a religious fanatic!!!

Often, they simply refuse to remove the coat of their religiosity that they have woven for themselves over years of religious practice. Perhaps Jesus would make the same remark to them as he made to the Pharisees in Jerusalem:

"When he came near to the place where the road goes down the Mount of Olives, the whole crowd of disciples began joyfully to praise God in loud voices for all the miracles they had seen: 'Blessed is the King who comes in the name of the Lord! Peace in heaven and glory in the highest!' Some of the Pharisees in the crowd said to Jesus, 'Teacher, rebuke your disciples!' 'I tell you,' Jesus replied, 'if they keep quiet, the stones will cry out.'" (Luke 19 vs 37 – 40)

I often say to myself that the only things that people agree to take off to get into the river of the Spirit are their shoes. These same shoes that give zeal for the Gospel, Ephesians 6 vs 15.

Those who accept having water up to their knees.

The deeper it gets, the more the temperature drops and the less enjoyable the dip becomes. This is what stops people in their walk with the Holy Spirit. The deeper we want to go with Him, the more the Spirit of God will reveal things in our lives that we need to reform. And that is not enjoyable. Many people take a step back when the Holy Spirit starts revealing too much about their lives, instead of continuing and being washed in the blood of Jesus! It's like the followers who left Jesus when they found His words becoming too tough. (John 6 vs 66)

The problem with these people often comes from the fact that in order to go deeper into the river, it will require removing the rest of our clothes. And especially that beautiful jacket on which we have pinned all our medals. The one for our water baptism, the one for our baptism in the Holy Spirit, the one for when we really came to accept giving our full tithe, etc. Thus, we find ourselves naked before the Lord, but also before all the people we were subconsciously trying to impress.

The Holy Spirit wants to work not with people covered in medals or degrees, but with people full of humility! Agreeing to go deeper in the river means agreeing that we will allow ourselves to be led, we who thought we would lead others. It is accepting not to be the leaders but to be "the led". It is accepting what, in our society, is often unacceptable: being dependant! (John 21 vs 18)

Those who do not want to lose their foot-hold.

When Ezekiel reaches the middle of the river, he says that at this point, the current is so strong, it is not possible for anyone to stand. Many say, at this point, that they will not go deeper because they cannot accept losing control of their lives. They are afraid of being manipulated.

But there is nothing more wonderful for a Christian than to be manipulated by the Holy Spirit. He will never do it against our wishes in any case, but His desire is that we abandon ourselves completely in His hands. This is the condition for us to be able to declare, as the Apostle Paul:

1 Cor 7 vs 22: *"For he who was a slave when he was called by the Lord is the Lord's freedman; similarly, he who was a free man when he was called is Christ's slave."*

What is the point of losing one's foot-hold? Many ask this question and wonder to themselves: why does God move in this way? What is the point of laughing, for example? I think there are several answers to these questions.

The first relates to what we have already explained: God moves in a way that confounds the wise. In fact, the Lord does not like those kinds of questions if they are asked with the attitude of "Why are You moving in this way? Is this normal?" The person who asks these questions with that kind of attitude already belongs to the type of people God wants to confound.

The second is that God does not make people laugh for the sake of laughing, nor does He make people cry for the sake of crying; He does not make people dance for the sake of dancing or make them fall for the sake of falling, etc. It is His way of healing, of delivering, of filling people with His joy; these things are God's therapy. They cause a positive result in those who are visited by God in this way.

Just because they might seem to be crazy at first to the wise of this world, doesn't make them less logical. Any doctor will tell you that laughing is constructive and has a restorative effect on people.

Joy in the Holy Spirit is not just inane silliness; His joy changes things in its wake. Look at times of revival: in that day, says Zechariah, *"Grain will make the young men thrive, and new wine the young women."* Zechariah 9: 17. These manifestations of the Spirit will give birth to positive things: they will cause you to grow spiritually if you know how to use them beneficially.

Things in the physical world: dancing, singing, laughing, weeping, trembling etc… have an equivalent in the spiritual world. We find it absolutely normal for a whole hall of people to burst out laughing if they are listening to a comedian; yet it shocks us when it comes to things of the Spirit because we don't understand that the Holy Spirit has the right to cause the kind of joy in us that makes us laugh.

When the Lord brought back the captives… our mouths were FILLED WITH LAUGHTER… (Ps126 vs 1 – 2).

Joy is a very important thing in the Word of God:

Romans 14 vs 17: *"For the kingdom of God is not a matter of eating and drinking, but of righteousness, peace and JOY IN THE HOLY SPIRIT."*

Nehemiah 8 vs 10: *"… the JOY OF THE LORD IS YOUR STRENGTH."*

There are anointings of joy: *"…and to bestow on them … THE OIL of gladness instead of mourning."* (Isaiah 61 vs 3), (Isaiah 51 vs 11): *"… everlasting joy will crown their heads. Gladness and joy will overtake them…"*

Hebrews 1 vs 9: *"… God, your God, HAS ANOINTED YOU with the oil OF GLADNESS…"*.

In Zechariah 10, we find again the spring rains and their consequences: *"Ask the Lord for RAIN IN THE SPRINGTIME…*(vs 1), and then some of the consequences of that rain, it says in verse 7, *"their hearts will be AS GLAD AS WITH WINE."*

My aim in this chapter is to point out that our recognition and understanding of the ways of the Holy Spirit are far from perfect. So rather than carrying on talking and being controversial about Him, let us allow ourselves to be taught by Him and commit ourselves to Him in a personal relationship, as just like Jesus, and just like our heavenly Father, He is a complete person in His own right and part of the Trinity. He can show His nature to each person, the way He moves and all the things reminding us of what Jesus taught through His Word.

John 14 vs 26: *"But the Counsellor, the Holy Spirit, whom the Father will send in my name, will teach you all things, and will remind you of everything I have said to you."*

For this to happen, we have to recognise His voice.

John 10 vs 1 to 5: *"I tell you the truth, the man who does not enter the sheep pen by the gate, but climbs in by some other way, is a thief and a robber. The man who enters by the gate is the shepherd of his sheep. The watchman opens the gate for him, and the sheep listen to his voice. He calls his own sheep by name and leads them out. When he has brought out all his own, he goes on ahead of them, and his sheep follow him, because they know his voice. But they will never follow a stranger; in fact, they will run away from him because they do not recognise a stranger's voice."*

The best way to do this is by spending the maximum amount of time in His presence, by praying, by reading the Word of God that He inspired, by meeting together with brothers, because:

"Where two or three come together in my name, there am I with them." Matt 18 vs 20

BEIT TEHILLAH

Having committed to redoing PAUL'S third trip but the other way round, to Israel on our yacht "Indeed" (between August 2015 and October 2016), God gave us a new vision for the coming years.

It was broken down into three areas:

Firstly, to open a prophetic route between the south of France and Israel which would prepare Aliyah for Jewish people to go back to the land promised to them by our God according to Isaiah 11 vs 11-12. In this passage, we read that God planned to bring back His people to the land that He promised them irrevocably. *"In that day, the Lord will reach out his hand a second time to reclaim the remnant that is left of his people from Assyria, from Lower Egypt, from Upper Egypt, from Pathros, from the upper Nile region, from Elam, from Shinar, from Hamath and from the islands of the sea. He will raise a banner for the nations and gather the exiles of Israel; he will assemble the scattered people of Judah from the four quarters of the earth.*

Having opened this route in our yacht, in worship and intercession over 13 months, we continued the work by opening a house of prayer called "Beit Tehillah" on the island of Gozo (Malta).

Through this house of prayer, our desire is to prepare the Mediterranean basin, in the light of a prophetic word that the Lord gave me in July 2015:

The first will be last, and as the Mediterranean basin was the departure point for the expansion of the Gospel, it subsequently became one of the most closed places in the world.

Whether it be emigrants who drown in it in their attempt to escape desperate situations and war, religious superstition throughout its "Christian" coastline, corruption, drugs, holidaying and parties, "Sea, Sex and Drugs", Islam assassinating men, women and children in Arab countries, Mammon which has torn Greece apart, the Mediterranean today is prey to the darkness!

But where sin abounds, grace abounds even more and I am going to cause a great revival to happen, the revival that will be the herald of my return. The season is close at hand and I will put men and women in place to work there and to prepare the way. This revival will come only to the extent that a throne of worship is built for me, and where my house, once again, is a house of prayer. This is why I am sending you there."

Therefore, we believe that this revival will be the beginning of the triumphal return of Jesus Christ in Israel, and in order to prepare for this, churches need to go back to the fundamental elements of the faith and of its roots: Israel. Romans 11 vs 17 -24:

"If some of the branches have been broken off, and you, though a wild olive shoot, have been grafted in among the others and now share in the nourishing sap from the olive root, do not boast over those branches. If you do, consider

this: You do not support the root, but the root supports you... And if they do not persist in unbelief, they will be grafted in, for God is able to graft them in again. After all, if you were cut out of an olive tree that is wild by nature, and contrary to nature were grafted into a cultivated olive tree, how much more readily will these the natural branches, be grafted into their own olive tree!"

We believe it is urgent to remind the body of Christ and everyone in the Mediterranean of these realities, and to bring people to a real repentance (change in thinking) in this area.

Alyah of a whole people!

Alyah, a Hebrew word meaning ascent or spiritual elevation, is a term that has been much talked about in recent times, as much in the media as in the church. In its most common use, it means the literal act of immigration to the Holy Land (Eretz Israel, in Hebrew) by a Jew. Such Jewish immigrants are called Olim.

On the other hand, if a Jew emigrates out of the land of Israel, it is called *Yérida*, literally meaning descent.

For many people, and particularly Christians, Alyah is a prophetic sign of the last days. In reading Isaiah 11 vs 11- 12, we read that God planned to bring His people back to the land that He promised them, irrevocably. *"In that day, the Lord will reach out His hand a second time to reclaim the remnant that is left of His people from Assyria, from Lower Egypt, from Upper Egypt, from Pathros, from the upper Nile region, from Elam, from Shinar, from Hamath and from the islands of the sea. He will raise a banner for the nations and gather the exiles of Israel; He will assemble the scattered people of Judah from the four quarters of the earth."*

Today, my aim is not to study the aspect of Alyah of the return of the Jews to their land from a political or even factual point of view, but rather, to approach it from a spiritual perspective.

Alyah, the ascent of all people, Jews and Christians, united as one New Man, towards their God!

When I was praying with my wife in Sardinia a few years ago, we had this thought. Cathy saw a hill high up, with three crosses on it (the ones from Golgotha?). But what was surprising was the stream of people gathering on this hill. It looked as if there would never be enough space for them all, yet when we got closer, we saw that there was still a lot of space ... space for everyone!

When she shared with me what she was seeing, I too saw it, and there were two columns of people going up each side of the hill, and this is how I understood it:

The cross in the middle was obviously Jesus, Yeshua's cross, the son of God, who died for our sins and rose again! There is salvation only through Him, claimed by the apostles and claimed by myself too.

This is true for the Jews: *"Then Peter, filled with the Holy Spirit, said to them: 'Rulers and elders of the people. If we are being called to account today for an act of kindness shown to a cripple and are asked how he was healed, then know this, you and everyone else in Israel: It is by the name of Jesus Christ of Nazareth, whom you crucified but whom God raised from the dead, that this man stands before you completely healed. He is the stone you builders rejected, which has become the cornerstone. Salvation is found in no-one else, for there is no other name under heaven given to men by which we must be saved.'"* (Acts 4 vs 8 – 12)

This is true for people from the nations: *"Remember that at that time you were separate from Christ, excluded from citizenship in Israel and foreigners to the covenants of the promises, without hope and without God in the world."* (Ephesians 2 vs 12).

The other two crosses on this hill, on the other hand, represented believers from the nations on the one side, and believers from Israel on the other, who were becoming one people by making their Alyah (their ascent) towards the top of this hill in order to return to their God.

I felt that the Holy Spirit was telling me that only an ascent again of Jews returning to their God, and also of the Nations turning back to their God (who has been one and the same God all the time, whatever generations of Jews and Christians may have thought) - only this will bring about the fulfilment of the word in Romans 11 vs 23 – 24: *"And if they did not persist in unbelief, they will be grafted in, for God is able to graft them in again. After all, if you were cut out of an olive tree that is wild by nature, and contrary to nature were grafted into a cultivated olive tree, how much more readily will these, the natural branches, be grafted into their olive tree!"*

It is true that today, we are seeing a greater and greater geographical and political Alyah of the Jewish people, as has been prophesied all through the Bible. This Alyah is the sign that Someone is coming for the church of Christ in the nations, and this church, too, must ascend spiritually:

1. Towards its God. (Intimate relationship through true worship);
2. Towards His word. (Revision of some of our theologies which have been "adapted" over the course of the centuries);
3. Towards its Jewish roots. (Without which we are just dead branches).

Alyah, a return to God and to His Word.

In what way am I telling you the church needs to return to God? We are Christians, saved by grace and born of the Spirit; we go to church (or we pray in our homes); at any rate, we have a personal relationship with God. Perhaps Jesus could then make the same response to us as He did to His generation: *"Abraham is our father,' they answered. 'If you were Abraham's children,' said Jesus, 'then you would do the things Abraham did.'"* (John 8 vs 39).

In what way are we different today to those people then? In fact, I believe that every time someone is caught red-handed, he denies it!

"Ever since the time of your forefathers you have turned away from my decrees and have not kept them. Return to me, and I will return to you,' says the Lord Almighty. But you ask, 'How are we to return?'" (Malachi 3 vs 7)

When I share with people how saddened I am about the gulf between what I read about the church of the book of Acts and what I see in the church today, most of the time, I get no reaction, or I get slightly strange explanations about how miracles were only there for apostolic times… or other excuses in the same vein.

But never, or at least very rarely, do I see people analysing themselves or challenging themselves to answer this question. We are like the people who kept trying to argue with the Lord in the book of Malachi!

We have distanced ourselves from God, we have grieved the Spirit, we have lost sight of the reason for the church's existence, by substituting it for a kind of club where we are waiting for Jesus to return. And we deny that there is a problem!

"If my people, who are called by my name, will humble themselves and pray and seek my face and turn from their

wicked ways, then I will hear from heaven and will forgive their sin and will heal their land." (2 Chron 7 vs 14)

When are we going to understand? When are we going to go to the Lord with a contrite heart rather than full of excuses?

We proclaim loud and clear that Jesus is God and that we belong to Him. We lean strongly on verses like these:
"In the beginning was the Word, and the Word was with God, and the Word was God. He was with God in the beginning. Through him all things were made; without him nothing was made that has been made. In him was life, and that life was the light of men. The light shines in the darkness, but the darkness has not understood it." (John 1 vs 1 – 5)

Jesus is the Word! Jesus is God! we profess! And yet I am flabbergasted to see how many Christians do not know basic teachings of Christ, the Word!

They are, however, capable of defending certain whacky "theologies" tooth and nail (How should one fall in the Spirit? Face-down or on one's back do not signify the same thing! The legal length allowed for hair or pants or sleeves…) and sometimes, even dangerous ones (replacement theology, forbidding communion or baptism based on the decision of a pastor, excommunication…)

Many people spend hours combing the Bible to define the date and time of Jesus' return; others to justify unacceptable behaviour in their religious practices; others still to justify the weakness of the church in the world, the absence of miracles, sick people and people dying in the midst of us…

Yet the most important message of the Word is shoved under the mat, without anyone being terribly upset about it!

"A new commandment I give to you: Love one another. As I have loved you, so you must love one another." (John 13 vs 34)

Instead, we have learnt to despise the other members of the body. We are so disinclined to love each other today, to be united, to march in the same army, the army of the King of kings, that we are experiencing exactly what the apostle Paul explained to the Corinthians as we saw at the beginning of this book.

Last summer, when we learnt that several of our Christian friends or their children had been hit by various cancers or other serious illnesses, my wife shared a very strong thought that she had received from God.

Whilst we were praying for these friends, she realised that there was a breach in the church through which sickness and death was able to come in! It was not the fault of the particular friends we were praying for; rather, it was the fault of the Body as a whole, incapable of making the commandment of Christ's love a priority!

The body of Christ is made up of all who have believed, without exception! *"So in Christ we who are many form one body, and each belongs to all the others."* (Romans 12 vs 5)

"Is Christ divided?..." (1 Cor 1 vs 13) This is the question Paul asked the Corinthians and that Jesus asks us today.

"In the beginning was the Word..." We are quite happy to recognise that this first verse of John speaks of Jesus. This Word, incarnate, came to offer Himself on a cross. As in the vision of the hill I described at the beginning of this chapter, we need to return (make our Alyah) to the cross of Christ and put into practice this grace that has been given to us.

Alyah, a return to our Jewish roots for a better understanding of the Word.

Not taking into account the Jewish roots of our Christian faith is like a person who knows nothing about China, other than Peking duck, reading a book several thousand pages long in Mandarin!

Heaps of absurd things have been said or done because of our misunderstanding of the Jewish context in which the Bible was written.

Someone said to me once, and I quote: "When Jesus was on earth, the Jews lost their chance of seeing the promises of God accomplished concerning them; today, those promises are null and void for them; they have become a reality for us!" My reply was this: "If God has changed His mind about the eternal promises He made to His people, the apple of His eye, how can I be sure He will not change His mind about the promise He made me: *"if I believe in His son, Jesus, I will not perish but will have eternal life"*?

The Bible tells us that in Christ, there are no longer Jews or Greeks. But those who are not in Christ will remain Jews or Greeks. In the same way, then, the promises made by God to the Jews will remain. We read one of these promises here: *"'I will establish my covenant as an everlasting covenant between me and you and your descendants after you for generations to come, to be your God and the God of your descendants after you…'*
*Then God said, 'Yes, but your wife Sarah will bear you a son, and you will call him Isaac. I will establish my covenant with him **as an everlasting covenant** for his descendants after him.'"* (Genesis 19 vs 7, 19)

We find this term everlasting (עולם, olam in Hebrew) **439** times in **414** verses in **34** of the books of the Old Testament. The definition of "everlasting" sadly seems to escape some people. Allow me, then to state it again here: forever, for good, continual existence, everlasting, eternal, that will never stop, indefinite future or without end, eternity.

One of the reasons that has pushed Christians to distance themselves from the love and unity commanded by Christ, which we spoke of in the last section, is the westernisation of the gospel, practised by the Roman Empire. In fact, this westernisation of the gospel was founded on a world view developed by the Greek philosophers, and it works on a binary system (Dualism), Plato's idea, and became the starting point of all subsequent philosophical theories on what is known today as Dualism.

This fundamental western way of thinking is not able to find a place for a trinitarian-based (three-part) way of thinking, which is the basis of all Hebrew thinking. Indeed, how is it possible to fit "trinity" into a system in which there are only two empty spaces?

It is thus hardly surprising that for many western Christians, the Holy Spirit is more a sort of "energy" than a whole person in His own right, what with the two open spaces in our western way of thinking having already been filled by the Father and the Son... It is not surprising, either, that most people confuse the soul and the spirit, as there again, defining humankind as being made up of three parts becomes culturally too complicated for western minds.

This way of thinking has led us to believe that since Israel rejected Christ, Christ has no option but to reject them too. It's either black or white! Paul must have struggled with this way of thinking, as we have seen above. (Romans 11)

Today in our meetings, we often read the Bible in a way that detaches it completely from the "trinitarian" culture and vision of those who wrote it. Often, we try to squash the Hebraic vision of the world into our (culturally dualist) way of thinking. This has led us to gloss over passages without understanding them, fitting them into Greek calendars when they are studied, probably in an attempt to give them a meaning that gels with our understanding, but which actually has nothing to do with the author of the text (who, as it happens, is God Himself).

Let's look at an example that illustrates the danger of not understanding a passage in the way intended by the author. For many people, the Ten Commandments represent the very essence of the Judeo-Christian way of thinking. Right from the start, we are misunderstanding the words!

The word Decalogue in Hebrew is literally translated: the ten words!

And the first word begins like this: I AM THE LORD YOUR GOD! Everything else rests on the fact that we have an eternal God, who does not vary and does not change and is the one who delivers us! *"I am the Lord your God, who brought you out of Egypt, out of the land of slavery."*

Let us now look at one of these words from the Decalogue:" Honour *your father and your mother, so that you may live long in the land the Lord your God is giving you."* (Exodus 20 vs 12)

The wrong understanding of this passage leads many Christians to an impasse. How, actually, can one honour a parent who lives in a way that opposes what God asks? I personally suffered for many years because of a chronic misunderstanding of this verse.

Yet there seem to be flagrant examples of disobedience to this commandment in the Bible that don't appear to bother God very much...

Judges 6 vs 27:" *So Gideon took ten men from among his servants and did as the LORD had said to him. But because he feared his father's household and the men of the city too much to do it by day, he did it by night."* (NKJV)

Then in 2 Chronicles 15 vs 16 – 18, we have a king, Asa, who in order to honour God, had no choice but to dishonour (remove the honour of) his mother, because his heart was fully committed to God, and the result of this was great blessing!

"Also he [King Asa] removed Maachah, the mother of Asa the king, from being queen mother, because she had made an obscene image of Asherah; and Asa cut down her obscene image, then crushed and burned it by the Brook Kidron. But the high places were not removed from Israel.

Nevertheless the heart of Asa was loyal all his days. He also brought into the house of God the things that his father had dedicated and that he himself had dedicated: silver and gold and utensils." (NKJV)

In our dualist way of thinking, too often we have confused the fact of *"honour your father and mother"* and have venerated them in order to get from God *"a long life in the land"*. Yet it wouldn't cross our minds to honour someone whose actions are questionable as it wouldn't add up.

Should we have submitted to (honoured) the Vichy authorities who were handing over huge numbers of innocent Jews to the Nazis, or later on, to the people who ordered the massacre of innocent people during the terrible challenges of decolonisation?

Now, the Hebrew term for honour, *kavéd*, literally means "to give weight to". In Hebrew, honour designates the real value of something, estimated at its true weight. It can also be translated by "giving someone his just, rightful place". The place that is due to him!

The commandment, or the word, therefore, can be understood as follows: honouring our father and our mother, actually means recognising the just weight of how our parents raised us. This comes back to the idea of making a critical evaluation in order to recognise what was good, what was not quite so good and to assess our upbringing very frankly, but, at the same time, without judging those who did it.

This right to assess one's upbringing, with the first word being the yard-stick we use, *"I am the Lord your God, who brought you out of Egypt, out of the land of slavery,"* allows us to re-adjust how we act (as did Gideon and Asa in destroying the idols put up by their parents). The consequence of this will be *"that we will live long in the land that the Lord our God has given us."*

If we do not re-read the Word of God through the spectacles of the correct way of thinking and communication that was established between God and His people, we will not be able to understand nor please the one who declares, *"I am the Lord your God, who brought you out of Egypt, out of the land of slavery."*

Reading the Bible in this way has now led us to relook at our objectives and our priorities in the ministry.

A House of worship and intercession.

When we left Malta, on our way to Israel on our yacht, "Indeed", God told us that we needed to return to the islands and to establish a base there for our ministry in the form of a house of worship and intercession and a training centre to be used to prepare the Mediterranean for the vision that God gave us of a revival that would come to this specific region of the world.

The closer we got to Israel, the more precise and specific the vision for this place became:

To raise up prophetic worship: *"'But now, bring me a harpist.' While the harpist was playing, the hand of the Lord came upon Elisha and he said, 'This is what the Lord says…"* (2 Kings 3 vs 15 – 16).

To raise up intercession aimed at Alyah, to bring about the fulfilment of the prophecy in Isaiah 19 vs 24: *"In that day Israel will be the third, along with Egypt and Assyria, a blessing on the earth. The Lord Almighty will bless them, saying, 'Blessed be Egypt, my people, Assyria my handiwork, and Israel my inheritance.'"* While praying for this project, I was given this name: **Beit Tehillah.**

- o **Beit**, meaning house in Hebrew, is a place where you live.
- o **Tehillah** is one of the words that can be translated into English as praise and worship. It is a form of praise and worship that is based not on the fact that our situation is glorious, but that He is worthy of our worship.

We find this word again in Psalm 22 vs 1 and 2: *"My God, my God, why have you forsaken me? Why are you so far from saving me, so far from the words of my groaning? Oh, my God, I cry out by day, but you do not answer, by night, and am not silent. Yet you are enthroned as the Holy One; you are enthroned on the praises (Tehillah) of Israel."*

It is in this kind of praise that God is seated, enthroned in the midst of His people. He is not content just to be present! To be seated, enthroned speaks of exercising authority, judging, reigning! One is seated at a tribunal or at an assembly...

When we praise and worship God in this way, we are inviting Him to reign over us and over everything around us.

THE PURSUIT OF HAPPINESS

Finding happiness is one of, if not *the* most shared desire of humanity. To be happy is the often-admitted aim of each of us. Whilst few people would be able to give an accurate definition of it, the number of ways of finding this famous "Grail" are as numerous as they are more or less successful.

Seeking happiness is so fundamental to modern thinking that it features in the founding writings of democracy, such as in the declaration of independence of the United States: *"...that all men are created equal, that they are endowed by their Creator with certain inalienable rights that among these are Life, Liberty and the pursuit of Happiness"*.

This text expresses the values of "the enlightened" which are, or which seem to be, the basis of the rights of man and of authentic democracy, but our society, which claims these things, has not taken long to forget them.

Happiness resides in the spirits of all people, the ultimate ambition. And yet happiness can be harmful... in itself!

The authors of a recent study[2], exploring the consequences that happiness can have, affirm this point: happiness in itself should not be considered as universally and intrinsically good.

In practice, all types and degrees of happiness don't necessarily bring the same satisfaction. Seeking after happiness should, therefore, not be considered a major priority, nor even desirable, in cases where it leads people to feel worse than they did before.

June Gruber reminds us that the pursuit of a happy goal can turn around and bite you. Thus people who seek happiness at all costs, especially for themselves, can definitely feel less happy when they start looking for it.

This can be explained in failed attempts: when someone does not end up feeling as happy as they had hoped, it actually ends up having the opposite effect on them overall, and they become less happy.

In fact, systematic happiness can be a sign of a deficit of negative emotions, (sadness, guilt, shame) which, paradoxically, is not as desirable as it had seemed it would be at first.

As we have often seen in counselling, negative emotions are useful indicators for emotional and social relationships. For example, guilt reminds us to behave appropriately towards other people; fear prevents us from taking pointless risks, etc. So negative emotions, as much as positive emotions, are part of normal life.

[2] Published in "Perspectives on Psychological Science"

They are messengers that inform us about very real situations that need to be faced. If we kill the messenger under the pretext that he is not nice, before he even delivers his message, we will not be able to react to a situation that may well get worse.

The authors of the study remind the reader that for several years already, the field of psychology has discovered that the main engine of happiness, the most essential vector of the feeling of happiness is neither money, nor recognition because of success or fame. Quite simply, the feeling of happiness is linked to the ability to maintain significant social relationships.

This implies that the best way to find happiness seems to be to stop worrying about trying to find it! A better option, rather, would be to spend one's energy on strengthening and improving emotional and social connections, which are the real basis for a happy and psychologically "balanced" life.

And what if happiness is found without looking for it?

The pursuit of happiness for oneself (in other words, selfishly) often happens, to put it bluntly, to the detriment of others.

Let's go back to our declaration of independence of the United States. In its preamble, it speaks of the equality of all men and their inalienable rights - rights which the USA was quick to refuse to black and Indian people in order to provide Cupid-style happiness to a handful of white people.

This holds true for "the enlightened" who champion many things in their cosy living room discussions instead of getting their hands dirty by doing something concrete.

Still today, are we not like adulterers when it comes to our supposed belief in the "Universal Declaration of the Rights of Man" which we are all too ready to display at huge national conventions? Yet, to give an example from my own nation, we are very quick to turn a blind eye to our principles the moment it comes to selling our Airbus planes to totalitarian countries, in order to ensure the prosperity and happiness of France!

Does this make us happier? Allow me to suggest not. So while one study shows that Norway has topped the charts for being the most prosperous country in the world for many years, another study shows it to score the highest for nations using anti-depressants!

Yet surely standard of living, comfort, riches should at least contribute to one's happiness?

I think that depends on what we do with all of it. Often in my work, I have had the opportunity to see people who, in spite of all their possessions, never seem to manage to reach the happiness that they so covet. And there are others, deprived of everything, who always exude joy and take pleasure in sharing what they have.

The source of their joy is that they have always understood that there is greater happiness in giving than in receiving!

Here again, studies have shown, as we have seen, that it is in social interaction that we find fulfilment, value in our existence and happiness. To put it differently, it is when I make someone else happy that I feel really happy myself.

Let's now look at this principle within a more spiritual framework.

And the key of happiness was:

John 15 vs 12: *"My command is this: Love each other as I have loved you."*

We often speak of the Ten Commandments, and actually, this name is not correct. For the Jews, they are known as the Ten Words of God. Words that God gave for a simple reason: if we abide by them, we will find happiness!

Could it be, then, that this ultimate commandment of Christ to love each other might be the key to happiness? That, indeed, there is more joy in giving than in receiving?

One day, a young man from our church explained to me that he was going to leave because he felt he was not receiving anything from being among us anymore. He admitted that he had received much over the years, but now, he needed to move on if he wanted to receive more. What seemed obvious to him saddened me a lot, because I am enormously fond of the young man and it really pained me to see him go. I comforted myself, however, by telling myself that if it was, in fact, true that I had nothing more to offer him, perhaps it would be better for him to go elsewhere.

However, after thinking about it for a few days, I asked myself the same question in a different way. Does it make sense to leave a church under the pretext of it not giving us enough (for our liking)? Wouldn't it make more sense, rather, to ask myself the question what I can bring to the church?

A bit like John Kennedy in his inaugural speech of January 1961: *"My fellow citizens of the world: ask not what America will do for you, but what together we can do for the freedom of man."*

The question deserves to be asked, then: Are we called to receive our whole life long and become mere consumers of God's dispensations? If we spend our entire existence as those who take and expect to receive, the inevitable result will be that we miss God's plan for our lives – to become collaborators in His Kingdom. After all, does God not expect us to worship Him?

And to turn away from our idols (the biggest of the lot being our ego) to serve Him, the living God?

This helps us, then, to understand those verses that encourage us to put up with injustices rather than being a bad testimony. The Bible invites us to rejoice when we are beaten for the Gospel and even to give our lives for the Kingdom of God and to consider it an honour. Paul even goes so far as to consider that our death would be an advantage!

But all of this asks us for a maturity that sadly we see very little in the church today, particularly in the west.

We need to grow!

The apostle John speaks to us about this growing into maturity in his epistle: 1 John 2 vs 12 – 13: *"I write to you, dear children… young men… fathers."*

It is part of the normal pattern for human beings to go through the different stages of their lives, which means physical, emotional and spiritual. When these stages are not experienced in their right order, psychiatry speaks of deficiency!

The writer to the Hebrews also tells us of the necessity to grow spiritually and to reach maturity that is in line with what we have received. He is surprised at the slow growth of people, or even their regression.

Hebrews 5 vs 11 – 12: *"We have much to say about this, but it is hard to explain because you are slow to learn. In fact, though by this time you ought to be teachers, you need someone to teach you the elementary truths of God's word all over again. You need milk, not solid food!"*

Paul gives a very frank explanation for slow spiritual growth in his first letter to the Corinthians in chapter 3 vs 2 - 3: *"I fed you with milk and not with solid food; for until now you were not able to receive it, and even now you are still not able; <u>for you are still carnal</u>..."* (NKJV)

Years after their conversion, the people that the apostle Paul is writing to are still on milk! Let's think about what this lack of spiritual growth implies by looking at the physical development of human beings.

Being on milk means being an infant, who, by nature, can only think about himself. He is at a stage where he expects the world outside to give him all due attention, and is not conscious of the world around him.

Then as he gets older, he learns, for example, when he is left to cry in his cot or when every whim is not attended to, that he is not the centre of this world that he is beginning to notice. Later on, through a process of socialising, he begins to realise that others also have legitimate needs. Thus, he has to learn to face up to his own frustrations in relation to others.

These frustrations, which are a key element in his learning process, will have to be managed for his whole life. That is what becoming an adult means.

Spiritually, it is the same. A Christian who stays on milk thinks that the world (or the church) revolves around him and his needs. If this can be coped with for a certain time, it certainly cannot last forever! The new convert needs to become able to look after himself more and more, so that the church will be able to look after the new ones coming in. In fact, there will also come a time when the church will need to count on him for help in the life of the church. One day, he will be the one who becomes the parent.

When I became a dad, it was one of the best days of my life. And this is what it will be like for everyone who turns away from his quest for happiness in order to become a blessing to other people.

This is also true in our praise and worship. What is the proportion of our services that are truly directed towards addressing God? Twenty years ago, when I decided to weigh up this question very honestly, I came to the conclusion that, on average, in a two-hour church meeting:

- o 50 minutes to 1 hour was taken up by praise and worship (most of which was focussed on people's needs, rather than on God Himself).

- 10 minutes was taken up by announcements (for the people).
- 40 minutes was taken up by the sermon (for people again).
- 10 to 20 minutes were spent on prayers for the sick or different needs (for people).

Now of course, all of these are good things! But is this the worship that God is asking of us? Is it really God whom we are honouring here?

Here is the definition of worship: *Religious homage, given to a divinity or a holy person. Practices that are regulated by a religion, to give homage to the divinity.*

In fact, we are only worshipping when we pay homage to God. The rest, which is addressed to man, is good, without question, but it cannot be called "worship".

It is time for us to return to God to pay Him homage and, as in the example of Jesus, to return to Him with our hands empty! Hebrews 9 vs 12: *"He did not enter by the means of the blood of goats and calves; but he entered the Most Holy Place once for all by his own blood, having obtained eternal redemption."*

Hebrews 10 vs 19 to 22: *"Therefore, brothers, since we have confidence to enter the Most Holy Place by the blood of Jesus, by a new and living way opened for us through the curtain, that is, his body, and since we have a great priest over the house of God, let us draw near to God with a sincere heart in full assurance of faith, having our hearts sprinkled to cleanse us from a guilty conscience and having our bodies washed with pure water."*

TABLE OF CONTENTS

Page 7   Introduction

Page 11   What Is Worship?

Page 17   Coming out of Egypt

Page 31   Worship in Church Meetings

Page 47   Building the Temple

Page 67   The Cloud of God Comes

Page 77   Deeper in the River

Page 87   Beit Tehillah

Page 105   The Pursuit of Happiness

Page 117   Table of Contents

Unless indicated, NIV has been used for the English Bible references.

From the Author : In French.

- ➤ Quand Il reviendra il me trouvera debout.
  Édition AC Diffusion 1995, épuisée.
- ➤ Je te bâtirai une Maison.
  Édition AC Diffusion 1998, épuisée.
  Réédité/révisé dans la Collection Passeport
- ➤ Poursuivi par ta Grâce
  Édition Vraiment Libre 2003
- ➤ Passeport pour une nouvelle Identité
  en Christ !
  Deuxième édition chez BoD 2009/2017.
- ➤ Passeport pour une louange
  en Esprit et en Vérité
  Révision et Réédition chez BoD 1998/2018
- ➤ J'étais ailleurs.
  Edition BoD 2015

From the Author : In English.

- ➤ Chase by your Grace !
  Edition BOD 2016
- ➤ Passport for a New Identity in Christ
  Edition BOD 2017